yorktown 1781

the world turned upside down

BRENDAN MORRISSEY

yorktown 1781

the world turned upside down

Praeger Illustrated Military History Series

Westport, Connecticut
London

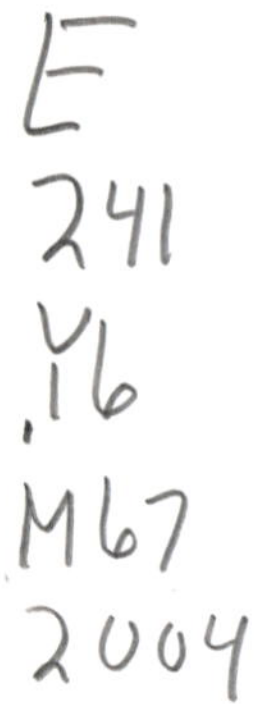

Library of Congress Cataloging-in-Publication Data

Morrissey, Brendan.
Yorktown 1781: the world turned upside down / Brendan Morrissey.
p. cm. – (Praeger illustrated military history, ISSN 1547-206X)
Originally published: Oxford: Osprey, 1997.
Includes bibliographical references and index.
ISBN 0-275-98457-5 (alk. paper)
1. Yorktown (Va.) – History – Siege, 1781. I. Title. II. Series.
E241.Y6M67 2004
973.3'37–dc22 2004050391

British Library Cataloguing in Publication Data is available.

First published in paperback in 1997 by Osprey Publishing Limited, Elms Court, Chapel Way, Botley, Oxford OX2 9LP. All rights reserved.

Library of Congress Catalog Card Number: 2004050391
ISBN: 0-275-98457-5
ISSN: 1547-206X

Praeger Publishers, 88 Post Road West, Westport, CT 06881
An imprint of Greenwood Publishing Group, Inc.
www.praeger.com

Printed in China through World Print Ltd.

The paper used in this book complies with the Permanent Paper Standard issued by the National Information Standards Organization (Z39.48-1984).

10 9 8 7 6 5 4 3 2 1

Illustrated by: Adam Hook

Key to military series symbols

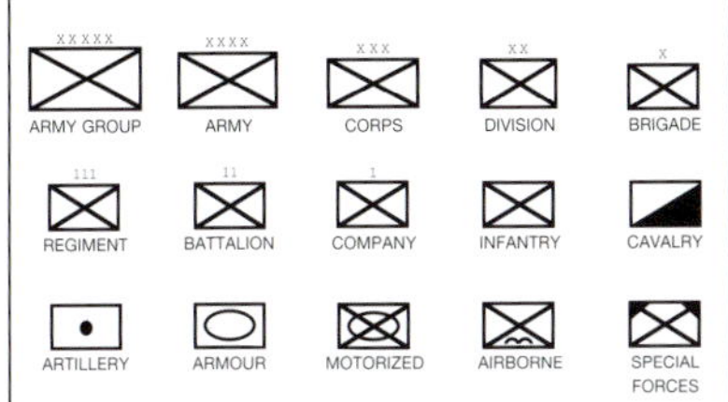

CONTENTS

COLONIAL NORTH AMERICA

Colonial North America showing the main cities and rivers, and the British garrisons confined to the coast and the Great Lakes.

THE ROAD TO YORKTOWN

On Thursday 28 June 1781, two officers and their escort of green-coated cavalry rode along a narrow peninsula in eastern Virginia, towards Chesapeake Bay. Their mission was to reconnoitre a small town, which stood on 35-foot-high bluffs at the north-eastern tip of the peninsula, overlooking the York River. The town had a harbour capable of accepting the largest merchant ships; two main roads led from it to Williamsburg and Hampton, 12 and 18 miles distant respectively, and a ferry crossed to Gloucester Point, a mile to the north-east. The surrounding land was gently undulating, with sparse vegetation – a few copses and the occasional plantation building were the only notable features. The soil was light and sandy, difficult to dig and easily eroded by wind and rain. Around the town ran two creeks – one a tidal, marshy cut with steep banks, to the west; the other, wider, to the south-east, with a mill pond at its head.

Coming under fire from artillery at Gloucester Point, the two officers agreed that the former tobacco port was not a suitable place to build the fortified naval base required by their commander-in-chief. As they rode away to look at other possible sites, they had no idea that little more than 100 days later, fate would bring them back to that same town, there to determine the futures of a nation and an empire.

Yorktown, by J Gauntlett, RN. Shown here in its heyday (around 1755), the town has been compressed slightly to fit into the view, and the wharves appear to be missing. Though Yorktown's prosperity had waned by 1781, the impressive houses on the bluffs above the river remained. Almost to a man, the merchants had supported the move toward independence, following Boston's lead with their own "Tea Party". The large building by the flag is the court house; the windmill at the far right is probably the one in Peale's painting of Washington and Rochambeau (on page 79). (Courtesy: Mariners' Museum, Newport)

THE WAR IN NORTH AMERICA: 1775-1781

By January 1781, Great Britain's struggle against her American colonies and their European allies had reached stalemate. The British presence in North America had been reduced to a mere handful of coastal bases, all surrounded by hostile countryside and under constant threat of attack, and a small field army in the Carolinas weakened by costly victories against a numerically superior foe. At the same time, Great Britain was having to fight virtually a global war against its imperial rivals, France and Spain.

The Americans, meanwhile, faced huge debts, shortages of every kind of military matériel, self-interested allies, mutinous rumblings among the troops of at least two states, and the general apathy of the population at large. It was not so much a question of who would win, as who would be the first to collapse.

Six years had passed since the New England militia had thwarted the raid on Concord and surrounded Boston, and an American attempt to seize Canada had narrowly failed. The following year, the British had left Boston for Halifax, where they were reinforced and, more importantly, retrained. By the end of 1776, one Anglo-German army had captured New York, forcing Washington and his shattered army into New Jersey, and another had cleared Canada, as part of a strategy to occupy the middle colonies and isolate the rebel heartland of New England. Meanwhile, the Royal Navy and Loyalists attempted to secure the South.

Washington's surprise attacks on Trenton and Princeton in the winter of 1776-1777, though no more than skirmishes against inferior numbers, gave the Americans new heart. Despite the defeats at Brandywine and Germantown, and the loss of Philadelphia, the capture of the Anglo-German army at Saratoga was the first clear-cut victory by either side, and encouraged first France, and then Spain, to enter the war. In 1778, a completely rebuilt Continental Army threatened Philadelphia and forced the British to retire to New York. Thereafter, there were no more pitched battles in the north, only raids by the Americans and French against British bases in New York and Rhode Island, and by Loyalists and Indians against New York and Pennsylvania. Meanwhile, in Virginia, a peace treaty with the local tribes, had left the Americans free to attack British posts on the western frontier.

Gloucester Point, by J Gauntlett, RN. Gloucester had also changed little since this sketch, made at the same as that of Yorktown, although by the time of the siege the woods behind the buildings had gone, either removed to allow the land to be cultivated, or used to construct the British defences. Note the windmill, just to the left of the three-masted vessel. During the summer of 1781, Gloucester was host to the American artillery unit, which fired on the two distinguished British officers conducting the reconnaissance of Yorktown. (Courtesy: Mariners' Museum, Newport)

Belatedly, the British looked to the South for aid, believing that it contained a 'silent majority' of Loyalists. If it ever had, they were now disillusioned by three years of neglect and the undivided attentions of local 'patriots'. However, the need for substantial reinforcements for the Caribbean and apathy at home meant that, real or not, the Loyalists had to be included in British plans.

At first, those plans were successful; in 1779, the British overran Georgia and held Savannah against a Franco-American force. In May 1780, they captured Charleston and its 6,000-strong garrison (the worst American loss of the war) before retiring to New York, leaving a small army to pacify the Carolinas. Yet despite another crushing victory at Camden and the occupation of North Carolina, the British were crippled by the loss of two important detachments at King's Mountain and Cowpens, and a pyrrhic victory over the reconstituted Southern Army at Guildford Court House. They were forced to abandon South Carolina, leaving only isolated garrisons for the Americans to mop up at will.

In July 1780, 5,000 French troops had arrived at Newport, which the British had abandoned the previous year. A mistake in the number of ships required left 2,500 more stranded in France, and a British blockade of Brest prevented them from ever sailing to America. With the disastrous record of Franco-American operations to date, the first task of this force was to regain the respect of their hosts.

THE GLOBAL POSITION IN 1781

Outside North America, the war had quickly become another episode in the struggle between European empires. Painstaking operations to capture each others' colonies were enlivened only by an inconclusive naval battle off Ushant and – almost inevitably – a siege of Gibraltar. Appreciating American sensitivities over Canada (and Catholicism), the French openly relinquished any aspirations in that area, but took full advantage of British commitments in America to attack India, Africa and the Caribbean, and only bad weather prevented invasions of Great Britain in 1778 and 1779.

Spanish efforts had concentrated on seizing Gibraltar, and capturing British outposts in the Floridas, Panama and the Caribbean. The first operation failed, despite French aid, and a Spanish fleet was badly beaten off Cape St Vincent in January 1780; the latter effort - though successful – was of no immediate help to the Americans. In fact, Spain gave no direct aid, being only too well aware of the perils of encouraging colonial rebellion, and hoping to expand its empire as much by diplomacy as by fighting.

In December 1780, Britain declared war on Holland (which had profited from American smuggling since the 1750s) and swept its fleets from the seas. The Dutch then joined the League of Armed Neutrality, formed in February 1780 by Russia, Denmark and Sweden to counter the seizure of neutral ships carrying American goods. By January 1781, Great Britain's only friends were a few land-locked German princes, some native tribes around the Great Lakes, and a dwindling (and increasingly disgruntled) band of Loyalists.

THE SEAT OF WAR

VIRGINIA 1775-81

Showing the operations by Dunmore's forces from the outbreak of war, and the

Virginia, named after the 'Virgin Queen', Elizabeth I, was the oldest and largest of the Thirteen Colonies, covering over 30,000 square miles and bounded on the north by the Potomac (or Patowmack) River, on the west by the 1763 Proclamation Line, and on the south by the boundary with North Carolina. To the east lay Chesapeake Bay, several miles wide for most of its 200-mile length, and leading to the Atlantic. The four major rivers – the James, York, Rappahanock and Potomac – were all capable of carrying large ships far inland and were fed by a network of creeks and minor rivers that made almost every plantation and town accessible by water.

The colonial government, dating from 1605, sat at Williamsburg, which had some 200 dwellings, but the largest town by far was Norfolk, with over 6,000 residents. In 1770, Virginia's population included 250,000 whites and 180,000 blacks; by 1780, numbers were 320,000 and 220,000 respectively. Only Massachusetts (which then included modern-day Maine) had a population even half as large. Virginia possessed almost half the slaves in North America, and the highest proportion of blacks to whites outside the Caribbean. This in turn shaped the colony's 'defence' policy: despite a widely dispersed population, the militia was constantly on the alert against slave revolts. Equally significant was the bellicose attitude of many Virginians, following disputes with Pennsylvania in the Ohio Valley, and native tribes opposing white expansion. (As recently as 1774, the Earl of Dunmore, the royal Governor of Virginia, had mobilised the western militia to deal with a Shawnee uprising.)

VIRGINIA IN THE REVOLUTION: 1775-1779

Although 'Dunmore's War' had temporarily united Virginia's political representatives, that unity had also facilitated their decision to support the New England colonies in their dispute with Great Britain. Dunmore responded by trying to seize the provincial powder supply at Williamsburg. When a 34-year-old lawyer, Patrick Henry, mobilised the militia, Dunmore outlawed him and threatened to arm the slaves. Peaceful counsel prevailed, but Dunmore feared being taken hostage and fled to HMS *Fowey*, from where he directed a series of raids by soldiers of the 14th Foot, who had been sent to restore order.

Throughout October, Dunmore seized or destroyed over 70 cannon, plus other munitions. On 7 November, he declared martial law, offering freedom to any slaves and indentured servants who joined him. With 100

subsequent raids by Mathew, Arnold and Phillips against major towns along the James River between 1779 and 1781.

regulars and 100 newly freed 'Loyalists', he marched to Great Bridge, 12 miles from Norfolk, causing 300 militia at Kemp's Landing to flee in panic. But the approach of the newly raised 2nd Virginia Regiment, under Col. William Woodford, forced him back to Great Bridge, where

ABOVE **Patrick Henry (1736-1799), after T. Sully. Famous for the phrase; 'Give me liberty or give me death!', this hot-headed lawyer of Scottish stock led the militant opposition to Dunmore. After the seizure of the rebel powder supplies at Williamsburg, Henry mobilised the local militia and later became commander-in-chief of all militia in Virginia, but was replaced when opponents exposed his lack of military experience. He resigned his commission and returned to politics, becoming Governor in 1779, and again after the war. (Courtesy: Independence National Historical Park, Philadelphia)**

he built a small wooden fort (christened 'the hog pen') to defend the causeway across the Elizabeth River, the main land route into Norfolk.

Learning that rebel artillery was coming from North Carolina, Dunmore decided to strike first, and on 9 December, 120 men of the 14th Foot attempted a dawn attack across the causeway. They were repulsed, losing 17 dead and 49 wounded, and with Woodford's force increased to 1,200, Dunmore abandoned Norfolk and transferred his men to a small flotilla he had assembled.

On 1 January 1776, Dunmore bombarded Norfolk, whereupon the garrison, frustrated by poor food and conditions, went on a two-day rampage, and abandoned the town on 6 February, burning the remaining houses to deny the British shelter (naturally, the British bombardment was blamed for all the damage caused and the 'Norfolk Incident' was cited as an argument for independence).

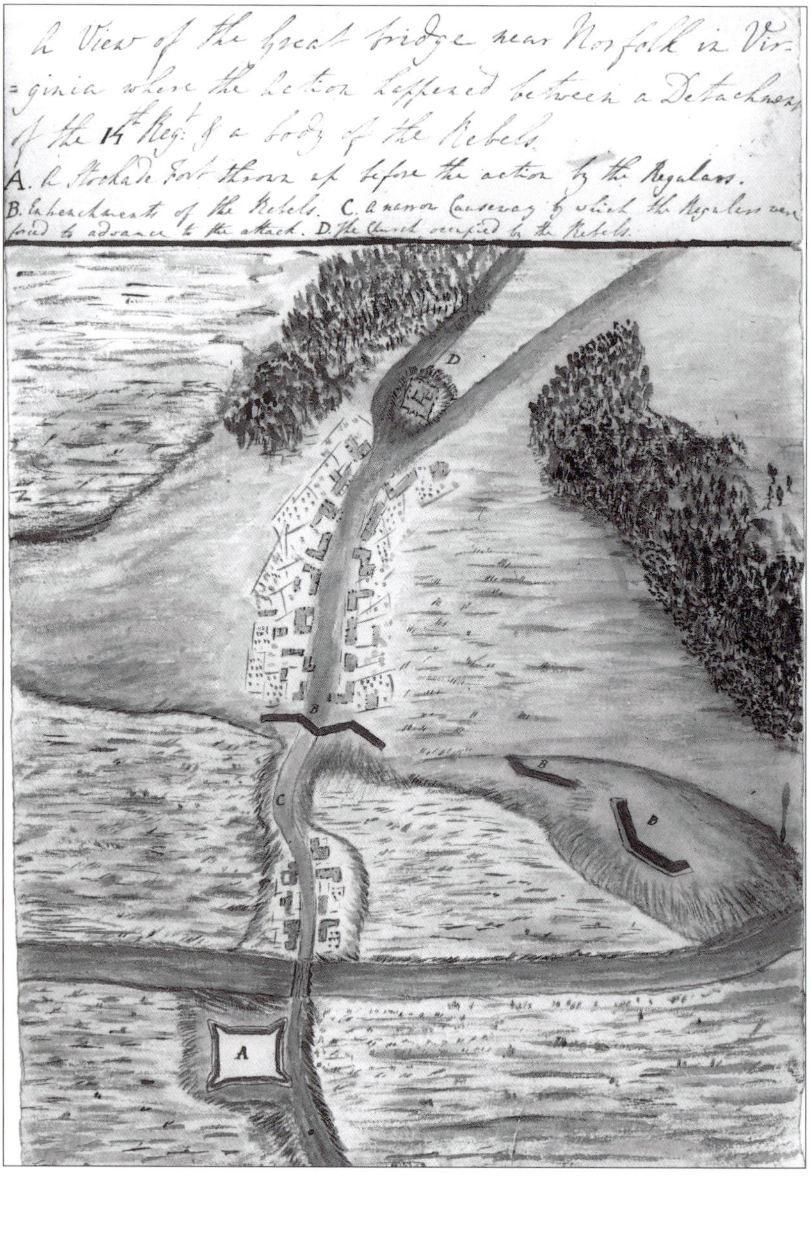

Depiction of the action at Great Bridge, by an unknown British officer. The river, surrounded by swamp, runs east-west; the road north-south. The American works ('B') are at the end of the causeway ('C') and on the high ground; they also fortified the church ('D') at the fork in the road. Dunmore's fort ('A') guards the south end of the bridge. (Courtesy: William L Clements Library, University of Michigan)

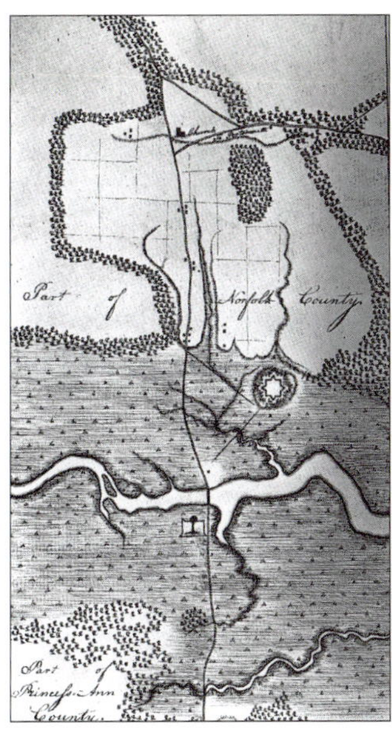

British fortifications at Great Bridge in 1781. These two maps show a more general view of the area around Great Bridge, which was an important crossing point over the Elizabeth River – possession would force an enemy to make a long detour through difficult countryside. The star fort in the right hand view held four guns and over 100 men, and was constructed between 5 and 9 February 1781 by the Loyalist legionary corps, the Queen's Rangers, during Arnold's raid. (Courtesy: Colonial Williamsburg)

Driven from successive bases by hunger and enemy manoeuvring, Dunmore was forced to cruise the Potomac, burning plantations and seizing supplies and water. Upon hearing of the abortive British attack on Charleston, South Carolina, he left Chesapeake Bay for New York on 5 August.

That December, Virginia's first General Assembly ordered natives of Great Britain not 'friendly . . . to the American cause' to leave as soon as possible after January 1777.

As the war progressed, the British viewed Virginia, with its fertile soil, easily navigable waterways, and remoteness from the main theatres (British and German prisoners from Saratoga were held in Charlottesville to prevent their recapture) as being vital to the American war effort. Virginia helped feed the Main and Southern armies, traded tobacco (its main crop) in Europe for arms and clothing (which it then stored in its arsenals) and was a prime source of horses.

Nevertheless, Virginia began to feel the pinch and Governor Thomas Jefferson had to ban the export of meat and grain, and compulsorily purchased surplus food at set prices to meet the army's needs. Militarily, the lack of British activity made the government complacent and the defence of the colony was neglected in favour of expeditions against British outposts and native villages to the west. When the British did turn their attention to Virginia, they exposed this weakness.

Thomas Jefferson (1743-1826), by C W Peale. Another lawyer, Jefferson was a poor orator, but a renowned literary draughtsman. His extremist writings prior to 1775 earned the respect of many radicals and he became the principal author of the Declaration of Independence. Succeeding Henry as Governor of Virginia in 1779, he was indecisive in office, a failure exposed by the British raids. Allegations of military unpreparedness (and personal cowardice) did not prevent him becoming a Peace Commissioner, ambassador to France, and later the 3rd President of the United States of America. (Courtesy: Independence National Historical Park, Philadelphia)

THE TOBACCO RAIDS 1779-1781

Benedict Arnold (1741-1801), by A Cassidy. No authentic portrait of Arnold is known, but this (tentatively identified) appears to show the characteristic beaked nose and heavy jaw. Made a brigadier-general following his defection, he was active in the destruction of American supplies in Virginia, but returned to New York before the Yorktown campaign. He then became an adviser on American affairs to the King, but financial insecurity always dominated his actions and he was no happier than in American service (where he was apparently the only major-general who was not a Mason). (Courtesy: Frick Art Reference Library, New York)

The first raid, a combined operation under Maj. Gen. Edward Mathew and Commodore John Collier, with 28 ships and 1,800 men[1], left New York on 5 May 1779, and arrived at Hampton Roads four days later. On 11 May they occupied the Norfolk Peninsula, seizing Portsmouth, Gosport (including Fort Nelson) and Suffolk, and capturing substantial naval supplies, ordnance and tobacco. The retreating Americans burnt a 28-gun warship under construction, and two French cargo ships with their loads. Over 140 more vessels were captured or destroyed, and the expedition returned to New York on 24 May, having inflicted £2,000,000 of damage without losing a man.

This success prompted the British commander-in-chief in North America, Lt. Gen. Sir Henry Clinton, to consider more raids (and his deputy, Lt. Gen. Charles, Earl Cornwallis, to consider occupying Virginia permanently). In October 1780, another raiding force, under Maj. Gen. Alexander Leslie, occupied Hampton Roads. Although Cornwallis (by now leading a separate force in the Carolinas) ordered it south to join him after the defeat of one of his detachments at King's Mountain, Leslie's arrival had still caused panic. The Virginia Assembly was forced to move the Saratoga prisoners to Maryland, and Maj. Gen. Nathaniel Greene – about to relieve Maj. Gen. Horatio Gates as commander of the Southern Army – had to leave Baron von Steuben in charge of the meagre Continental forces in the area. However, Jefferson continued to neglect the state's defences in favour of expeditions to the west – a policy that would cost Virginia dear and see him replaced as governor.

On New Year's Day, 1781, Benedict Arnold, now a major-general in the British Army, arrived in the Chesapeake with 1,500 men[2]. He had orders from Clinton to destroy supplies and force Greene to protect Virginia, thus relieving pressure on Cornwallis; he was also required to consult with Lt. Cols. Dundas (80th Foot) and Simcoe (Queen's Rangers), unaware that both had 'dormant' commissions to take over in the event of his 'death or incapacity'. (Ironically, his departure from New York on 11 December forestalled an American plot to kidnap him.)

Lieutenant-Colonel John Simcoe (1752-1806), by J L Mosnier. Simcoe joined the 35th Foot in 1771 and fought at Bunker's Hill. As a captain in the 40th Foot, he was wounded at Brandywine; taking over the Queen's Rangers, he was wounded again and captured, but exchanged in 1779. An independent officer, whose judgment was widely trusted, he was less flamboyant than Tarleton, but more professional. After the war he held governorships in Canada and the West Indies, and died en route to India after being appointed to succeed Cornwallis. (Courtesy: Metropolitan Central Library, Toronto)

Although a storm had delayed a third of the force, and killed half of the horses, Arnold still sailed 70 miles up the James River with the sloop *Swift* and the transport *Hope*, pausing only to capture a fort and put ashore his sickest men at Westover. He then marched 33 miles through the night, arriving at Richmond on the morning of 5 January. Taken by surprise, the militia and State Assembly fled and Jefferson was sent an ultimatum: allow British ships to remove all stores in Richmond (most of which was Loyalist property) and the capital would be spared. Jefferson either did not receive the demand, or refused to reply, so

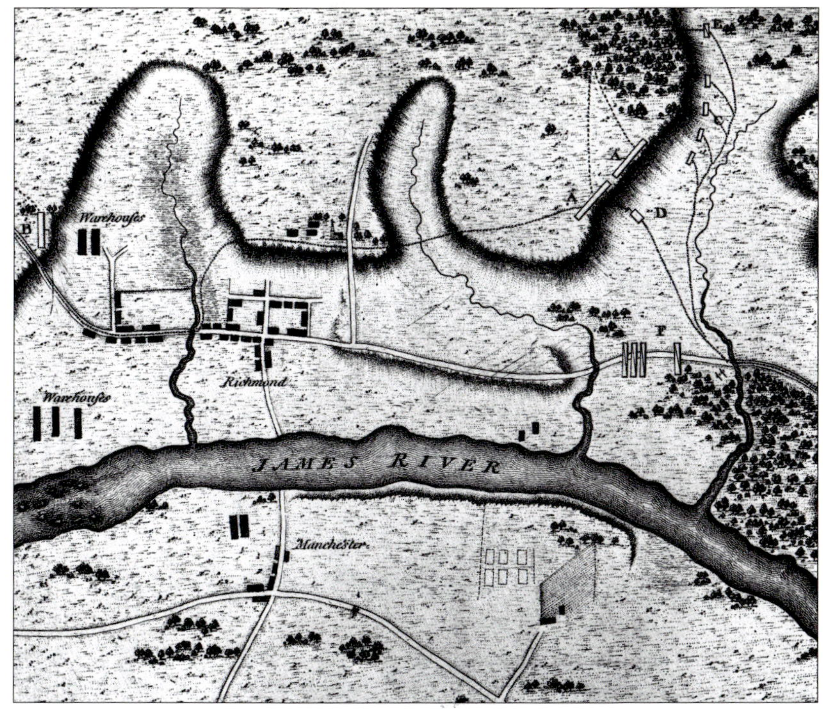

Skirmish at Richmond, 5 January 1781. One of a series of maps made for Simcoe from sketches by his officers. Despite being a small town of only 1,800 people (half of them slaves), Richmond's location made it a secure supply base, and led to it replacing Williamsburg as the seat of the Virginia government in May 1779. During Arnold's raid, Jefferson mobilised the local militia[4], but only 200 turned out and they were chased from Richmond Hill (as was a small party of cavalry to the west of the town) by the Queen's Rangers and Jaegers as the Governor watched from across the river, in Manchester. (Courtesy: Colonial Williamsburg)

Arnold ordered all military stores and food destroyed, and allowed local Loyalists to escape with shiploads of wine and spirits. Whether deliberately or otherwise, the fires started in public buildings spread and soon the whole town was ablaze.

Arnold then sent Simcoe seven miles up-river to Westham, to destroy a cannon foundry and clothing depot at Chesterfield. After two days, Arnold's force – which had not slept or eaten since landing – re-embarked and sailed for Portsmouth. Clinton ordered him to stay there, even though Jefferson had offered 5,000 gold guineas to anyone who killed Arnold, and he was the target of a pincer movement by a force of Continentals under Lafayette and von Steuben, and a French force from Rhode Island which had evaded the British blockade.

Luckily for Arnold, the Royal Navy caught the French and forced them back to Rhode Island on 16 March, and ten days later, Maj. Gen. Phillips – who had opposed Arnold at Saratoga – arrived at Portsmouth with 2,000 men[3]. On 18 April, the combined force moved up the James River, capturing Williamsburg and burning the Chickahominy River shipyard. Moving south to the Appomatox River on 25 April, they defeated von Steuben at Blandford and destroyed supplies at Petersburg, before attacking Osborne's Wharf on the James River on 27 April,

Major-General William Phillips (1731-1781), by F Cotes. Phillips entered the Royal Artillery in 1746, gaining fame at Minden and Warburg. He arrived in America in 1776, and – contrary to regulations – was given local major-general's rank as Burgoyne's second-in-command in the Saratoga campaign. Though admired by his captors, his behaviour forced them to place him under arrest until exchanged in 1780. He was one of Clinton's few trusted confidants and led expeditions to Rhode Island and Virginia before his death from typhoid fever. Despite their earlier 'meeting', he seems to have worked reasonably well with Arnold. (Courtesy: Frick Art Reference Library, New York)

sinking or capturing 20 ships of the Virginia Navy gathering to attack Portsmouth.

The next day, the British burned Chesterfield Court House and destroyed tobacco warehouses at Manchester on 30 April, but Lafayette's unexpected arrival at Richmond, with 1,200 Continentals, forced Arnold and Phillips to head back to Portsmouth. En route, they learned that Cornwallis was heading for Virginia, and they immediately turned back, landed at Brandon on 8 May, and marched to Petersburg to await his arrival.

Landing at Burwell's (Burrell's) Ferry, 17 April 1781. On Phillips' arrival in Virginia, the combined British force moved up the James River, detaching Simcoe's command to drive the militia from Williamsburg and seize Yorktown. Simcoe arrived at Burwell's Ferry, just below Williamsburg, to find the militia entrenched; bombarding the earthworks from a gun-boat, he landed his men down-river, where they soon outflanked the defenders, who fled (as they did from Williamsburg itself, the following day). After examining Yorktown, Simcoe reported that it would require a large garrison. (Courtesy: Colonial Williamsburg)

BRITISH STRATEGY IN THE SOUTH

Substantial success had been expected after the capture of Charleston in May 1780 – not least in London where the government of Lord North was well aware that the war was becoming increasingly unpopular throughout Great Britain. However this expectation remained unfulfilled largely because of the growing rift between the members of the British high command in North America.

Clinton believed that America could be pacified by the establishment of a chain of fortified posts at strategic coastal bases throughout North America, from which raids could be mounted against American

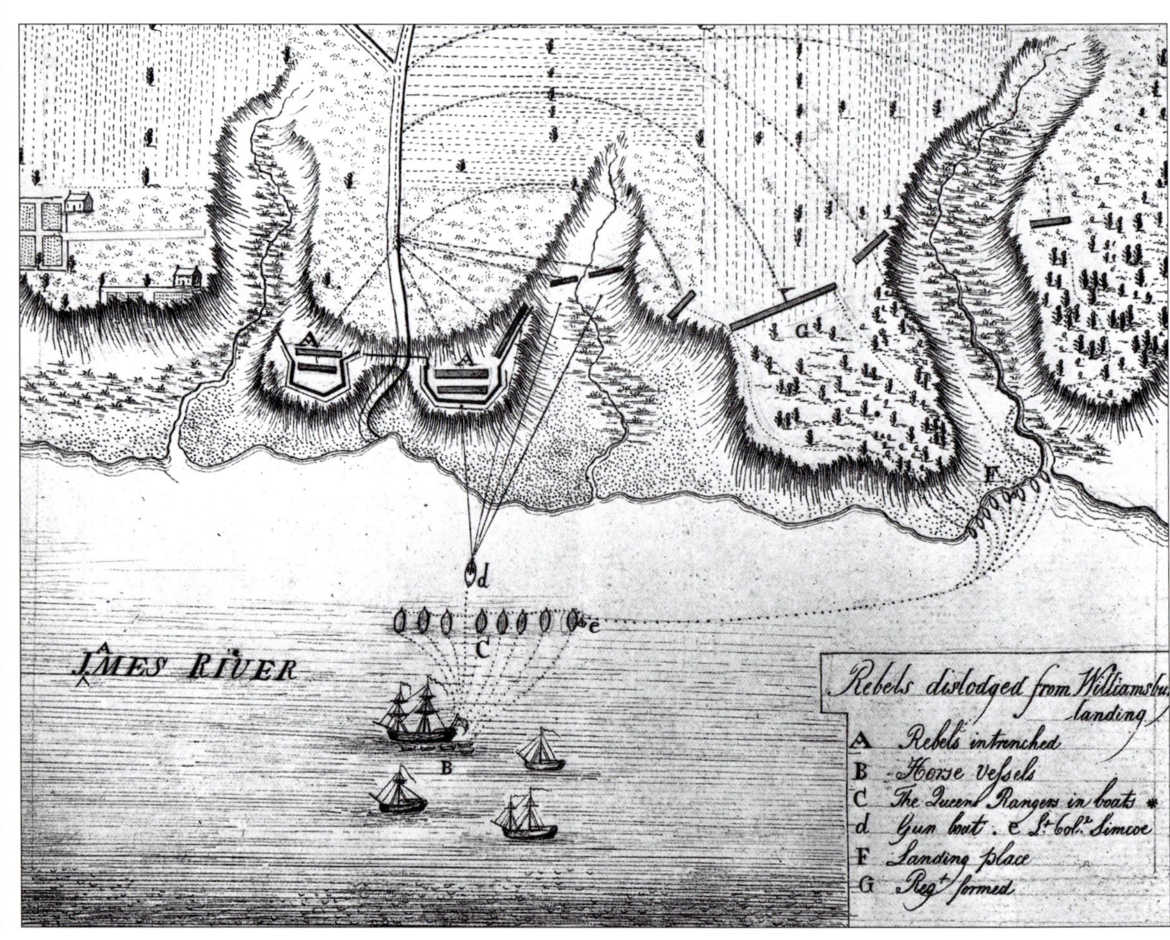

outposts. Although he also recognised that the security of these bases rested entirely on local naval supremacy, he – and others – appeared to assume that this would always lie in the hands of the Royal Navy.

Late in 1780, Clinton proposed the establishment of a naval base in Chesapeake Bay, from which to threaten the central colonies, and to strike at Philadelphia in conjunction with a thrust south by part of the New York garrison. When sending Phillips to Virginia, Clinton had made it plain that, while the priority was to support Cornwallis in the Carolinas, Phillips should be ready to support moves around the Chesapeake Bay and Delaware Peninsula. Cornwallis's brief was to hold Georgia and South Carolina, and to undertake offensive operations only where necessary to promote this aim. However, both parts of this strategy required the Royal Navy's support, and a commander with military ability and the tact to deal with Clinton. Unfortunately, the commander of the American squadron at that time, Vice-Admiral Marriot Arbuthnot, had none of the above qualities, and his squadron was under-strength, under-manned and poorly supplied.

George Sackville, Lord Germain (1716-1785), by T. Gainsborough. Son of the Duke of Dorset, and a graduate of Trinity College, Dublin, Sackville enjoyed considerable patronage at Court. He succeeded Lord Dartmouth as Secretary of State for the American Colonies in November 1775, and remained in that vital position throughout the war. A haughty manner, and other unpleasant traits, undoubtedly contributed to eventual defeat, by causing confusion among military commanders and under-estimating the abilities of the enemy. However, changes in the political scene after the war led to his being blamed unfairly for every shortcoming of the British war effort. Famous as 'the coward of Minden', he was actually court-martialled – at his own request – for disobeying orders; in fact, he had shown great personal bravery at Fontenoy, where he was wounded. He took the name 'Germain' in 1770 as a pre-condition of an inheritance. (Courtesy: Courtauld Institute, London, and Sackville-West family)

For his part, Cornwallis did not agree with Clinton's strategy (and even undermined it briefly by ordering Leslie to join him). He believed that the British should have as few posts as possible, but that wherever there was a force, it should be substantial. Despite the logistical problems of operating in hostile country hundreds of miles from British bases on the coast, he considered the pacification of the 'backcountry' of North Carolina was essential to defeat the last major American force in the South, and convince the hitherto elusive 'masses' of southern Loyalists that it was safe to show themselves.

Following the painful success at Guildford Court House on 15 March, Cornwallis retired to the port of Wilmington, North Carolina, from where he could be re-supplied and reinforced by sea. He also had the options of either marching back inland after Greene, rejoining the British garrison at Charleston, or taking the war into Virginia in order to severely disrupt the American supply network and split the colonies in two. Deciding that this last would be the most productive use of his forces, he wrote: 'Until Virginia is in a manner subdued, our hold of the Carolinas must be difficult, if not precarious.' He even suggested that Virginia might become 'the Seat of War . . . at the expense of New York'.

When Cornwallis entered North Carolina, he obtained permission from London to correspond directly with the Secretary of State for America, Lord George Germain, on the basis that Clinton, in New York, was too far away to control affairs. Clinton was unaware that Cornwallis's plan was gaining support in London, despite previous government approval of his own proposals, as there was no communication from Cornwallis between a letter of 18 January relating the Cowpens débâcle, and an optimistic report from Wilmington on 10 April concerning the 'victory' at Guildford Court House. In contrast, on 18 April, Cornwallis had written to Germain hinting that the British cause in the Carolinas was as good as dead.

THE OPPOSING COMMANDERS

THE BRITISH COMMANDERS

Much is made of the contribution to divisions in the British command structure, and eventual defeat, of the patronage and purchase systems that dominated the Army and Royal Navy at this time. However, the obsession of English politicians with the potential threat of a standing army resulted in the officer corps being deliberately and inextricably tied into party politics, preventing senior officers, however independently wealthy, from progressing without patronage. The inevitable *quid pro quo* guaranteed that they became political animals whether they liked it or not. In addition, they operated within a system geared, not to winning wars, but to minimising peacetime costs and maximising wartime profits for private contractors and public servants. Other individuals might (possibly) have done better, but they would have come from the same stable. Before applying 20th-century morality to 18th-century lives, it is worth remembering that the soldiers, sailors and politicians who lost Great Britain's American colonies emerged from a similar – in many cases, the same – society as that which produced their 'patriotic' opponents.

Lieutenant-General Sir Henry Clinton (1738-1795). Clinton and Cornwallis, though both 43 and ex-Guards officers, differed completely in temperament and in their views on winning the war. Clinton – forced to consider 'the big picture' and often hamstrung by the lack of co-operation from the Royal Navy – was always seeking to protect New York; Cornwallis – with only local responsibility – constantly sought the killer blow. While it is easy to criticise them, given the position in 1781, it is hard to imagine a strategy that could do more than delay the inevitable. (Courtesy: National Army Museum, London)

Lt. Gen. Sir Henry Clinton (1738-1795) was one of three major-generals sent to America in 1775 (see Campaign 37, *Boston 1775*) and succeeded Sir William Howe as commander-in-chief in North America, in 1778. His talents in the field – typified by the capture of Newport and Charleston – were too often submerged by an inability to give clear, concise orders and a sensitivity to criticism (the latter possibly exacerbated by depression following his wife's death). Ironically, the man who was such a difficult deputy for Howe was in turn plagued by the politics and failings of his own subordinates (especially Arbuthnot, the naval commander). This, with government interference and some appalling bad luck, led him to offer his resignation several times in the final years of the war. Disconcerted by the 'dormant commission' of Cornwallis (which was actually intended to ensure that a British, rather than German, officer would succeed as commander-in-chief), he increasingly felt it was more politic to make recommendations or requests to him, rather than give direct orders.

Clinton undoubtedly had a better grasp of what was viable in North America than many contemporaries – although even he failed to see, until too late, how vulnerable isolated posts and corps could be if the enemy had local naval superiority. He certainly laboured under the handicap of being expected to achieve as much as his predecessor, but with inferior numbers, decreasing support from the Royal Navy, and increasing intervention by the French. Though widely blamed for Yorktown, he was refused an enquiry to clear his name. A Member of

Parliament from 1772 to 1784, he was re-elected in 1790; he was made a general in 1793, and was Governor of Gibraltar when he died.

Lt. Gen. Charles, Earl Cornwallis (1738-1805), was a trusted courtier and, like Clinton, a former Guards officer. A Whig, he initially opposed Government measures to deal with the colonists, but agreed to serve in North America, seeing action around New York and commanding a division at Brandywine and Monmouth, before being made lieutenant-general in 1778. Given command in the South after the fall of Charleston, he used Clinton's remoteness (in New York) and the vague and contradictory nature of some of his superior's orders, as an excuse to pursue his own strategy.

Despite overwhelming Gates at Camden, Cornwallis was out-thought by Greene (whose strategic awareness and tactical limitations made them virtual opposites). Although he would be badly let down by the Royal Navy, his obsession with Virginia played a major part in ensuring that the surrender at Yorktown was crippling, yet he returned to England a popular figure. Cornwallis was not only personally brave, but also (except for one occasion in 1776) proved himself one of the ablest battlefield commanders on either side. Sadly, in America at least, his strategic abilities were found wanting, although he later achieved fame in India, where he eventually died. He was briefly governor-general of Ireland in 1798, but resigned over government refusal to grant Catholic emancipation.

Brig. Gen. Charles O'Hara (1740-1802), the only other general in Cornwallis's force at Yorktown, joined the army in 1752 and saw action in Germany and Portugal, before commanding a penal battalion in Senegal. He arrived in America in 1778 and, as a brevet colonel, led the Foot Guards detachment in the South, being wounded at Guildford Court House. Though somewhat garrulous and boastful, he was admired on both sides for his aggressive leadership and friendly manner. Promoted to major-general on being exchanged, he was captured at Toulon in 1793 and, ironically, was then exchanged for Rochambeau. He became Governor of Gibraltar, before dying from the effects of the wounds received in America.

Vice-Admiral Marriot Arbuthnot (1711-1794) was naval commissioner at Halifax from 1775 to 1778, before being appointed to command the American station in 1779. Old, lazy, unreliable and vulgar, his relationship with Clinton severely damaged the British cause. Having barely co-operated during the capture of Charleston, he allowed the French to occupy and fortify Newport, and prevented Clinton's attempts to attack them before they had completed the task. Through poor tactics and indecisive leadership, he failed to destroy the French fleet off the Virginia Capes in March 1781, and left for England in July to be replaced by Graves. He became an Admiral of the Blue in 1793.

Charles, Earl Cornwallis (1738-1805), by T Gainsborough. This well-known portrait was painted in 1783, shortly after his return to England. Cornwallis believed that direct action would bring victory – unlike Washington, who deliberately avoided pitched battles, except where he had overwhelming advantages. Though personally brave, popular with his men and a skillful tactician, Cornwallis failed to grasp the lessons learned by his various opponents, that merely winning battles would not win this particular war. (Courtesy: National Portrait Galllery, London)

Vice-Admiral Marriot Arbuthnot (1711-1794), by C Hodges. Arbuthnot's arrival in America, coming after repeated calls by Clinton for a competent commander for the North American squadron, was regarded by the latter as a personal affront. However, the admiral's lack of co-operation was not confined to the Army. In September 1780, he protested vehemently at being temporarily superseded by Admiral George Rodney, who had come from the Caribbean to prevent the French West Indies fleet giving the Allies the sort of local superiority that would prove decisive a year later. (Courtesy: National Maritime Museum, Greenwich)

ABOVE **Rear Admiral Thomas Graves (1725-1802), by J Northcote. Graves had more ability than Arbuthnot, but not of the sort required for independent command. He worked closely with Clinton and, unfortunately, shared the latter's cautiousness, especially regarding New York. However, in fairness to him and his predecessors, the North American squadron was invariably the 'poor relation' of Royal Navy commands, due to the anticipated threat – later realised – from France and Spain. (Courtesy: National Maritime Museum, Greenwich)**

RIGHT **General George Washington (1732-1799), by C W Peale. This famous portrait shows Washington with his aide-de-camp Tench Tilghman (right) and Lafayette (centre). Contrary to Revolutionary myth, Washington did not plan the Yorktown campaign months in advance – in fact, he favoured an assault on the main British base at New York. However, a Franco-American attack on Cornwallis in Virginia was one of several options available, if the French could guarantee local naval superiority. It was his ability to see this that gave the Allies the flexibility to take the opportunity when it appeared. (Courtesy: Independence National Historical Park, Philadelphia)**

Rear-Admiral Thomas Graves (1725-1802), was from a famous naval family and was a cousin of Samuel Graves (see Campaign 37, *Boston 1775*). Though court-martialled in 1756, he still attained flag rank in 1779, and was sent to New York to join Arbuthnot, whom he briefly succeeded as commander of the American squadron, following the action of 16 March. His indecision on 5 September allowed the French to reach the open sea, then retain control of Chesapeake Bay. Although he tried to work with Clinton, he was guilty of over-lengthy planning, and trying to cover every eventuality. Promoted to admiral in 1794, he was second-in-command at the Glorious First of June, where he received wounds that forced him to retire.

THE AMERICAN COMMANDERS

General George Washington (1732-1799) was a former militia colonel and farmer, but was chosen to lead the Continental army principally because he was a southerner. No tactician, he was frequently bested by Howe and Clinton in the field, yet he was essential to the American cause, being admired and respected by all ranks – personal rivals such as Charles Lee excepted. Strategically, he understood the necessity to avoid major actions, and to keep the American army in one piece – even in defeat. His ability to achieve this through the early years, and to reorganise when occasion demanded (as it all too frequently did) contributed to final victory. Skilful in dealing with an ally whose (often secret) agenda differed from his own, he could also delegate to subordinates, though he was luckier than Clinton in being able to choose – or at least recommend – his preferred candidates. After the war, he retired from public life, before serving two terms as president (and declining a certain third); ironically, his last military duty was to return to his former role as commander-in-chief in anticipation of war with France in 1798.

Maj. Gen. Marie Joseph Paul Yves Roch Gilbert du Motier, Marquis de Lafayette (or La Fayette) (1757-1834) joined the French army in 1771, and sailed for America with Baron de Kalb to serve without pay as a volunteer. Commissioned major-general (though without command), he was wounded at Brandywine and became Washington's protégé. Commanding Virginia's light troops, he survived the winter at Valley Forge, and fought at Monmouth and in the failed Franco-American attack on Newport. In 1779 he returned to France in triumph, and though his wilder schemes were rejected, he was instrumental in having Rochambeau sent to America. Though not overly talented, he succeeded in evading Cornwallis during his first independent command in Virginia, and later led the Light Division at Yorktown. Despite

subsequent romanticisation, and his own love of public adoration, he undoubtedly espoused the cause for which he fought, donating $200,000 of his own money.

Maj. Gen. Benjamin Lincoln (1733-1810) had been a town clerk, magistrate and farmer in Massachusetts before becoming a lieutenant-colonel, and later major-general, of militia. In 1776, for his part in defending New York, Washington recommended him for a Continental commission, and he played a prominent role in disrupting British supply lines during the Saratoga campaign (in which he was wounded). Commanding the Southern Department, he led the American contingent at the abortive siege of Savannah, and was captured at Charleston in 1780, later being exchanged for Generals Phillips and von Riedesel. He led the American wing of the army on the march to Yorktown and accepted the British surrender. He became Secretary of War for two years, and held a succession of civil posts until his death. Though more accomplished as an administrator than a general, he was a brave and respected leader.

ABOVE **Major-General Marquis de Lafayette (1754-1834). Regarded by Washington almost as a surrogate son, and given high command (controversially) while only in his mid-twenties. Lafayette did not particularly distinguish himself during the campaign in Virginia, but did manage to prevent Cornwallis from catching and destroying the only force of Continentals in that part of the country. On his return to France, he worked with Thomas Jefferson and held political and military posts in the French Revolution, but declined to serve Napoleon. He toured America in triumph in 1824, but again failed in French politics in the 1830s. (Courtesy: Anne S K Brown Collection, Providence)**

Maj. Gen. Friedrich Wilhelm Augustus von Steuben (1730-1794) was born in Magdeburg but raised in Russia. He served in the Seven Years' War, becoming an aide to Frederick the Great, but finished as the destitute chamberlain of a penniless German prince. Introduced to Washington by Benjamin Franklin, Steuben arrived in America in December 1777 and, with a hand-picked company, instructed the American army in European methods of drill. As major-general inspector general, he served in Washington's headquarters and liaised with Congress over the frequent re-organisations. After undistinguished service as Continental commander in Virginia, including the thankless task of rebuilding the Virginia Line and controlling the headstrong militias, he was in his element at Yorktown, where his views on siege warfare were deferred to throughout (the nearest he ever came to field command). After assisting with demobilisation, he was discharged in 1784 and spent his final years in poverty in New York. Probably overrated as a drill-master, his real value was his experience of the Prussian staff (a unique institution at that time). He was also renowned for generous hospitality to his subordinates, and an ability to swear in several languages.

General Thomas Nelson (1739-1789) succeeded Jefferson as governor of Virginia in June 1781, and commanded its militia in the Yorktown campaign. Initially moderate, he increasingly supported Patrick Henry and became colonel of the 2nd Virginia Regiment in 1775, before resigning to take Washington's place in Congress. An overweight asthmatic, he was still lively and alert, and commanded Virginia's armed forces from 1777,

LEFT **Major-General Benjamin Lincoln (1733-1810), by C W Peale. Although popular myth has it that Lincoln was allowed to accept the British surrender at Yorktown because of the way he was humiliated at Charleston the year before, it was in fact as Washington's second-in-command and thus the military equal of Brigadier-General O'Hara. (Courtesy: Independence National Historical Park, Philadelphia)**

organising the defence against British raids (effectively becoming a benign military dictator). Bankrupted by his support for the war (he aimed a cannon at his own house during the siege), he was buried in an unmarked grave to avoid creditors taking his body as security.

Major-General Baron von Steuben (1730-1794), by C W Peale. Despite being an imposter (in terms of representing his own military background), von Steuben undoubtedly helped mould the Continental Army into a fighting force – though perhaps less in his popular guise as a drillmaster than as an administrative adviser to Congress. In the absence of anyone more qualified, he became the 'oracle' for siege operations during the Yorktown campaign. (Courtesy: Independence National Historical Park, Philadelphia)

THE FRENCH COMMANDERS

Lt. Gen. Jean Baptiste Donatien de Vimeur, Comte de Rochambeau (1725-1807), joined the cavalry in 1740 and was a colonel at 22. He served at Minorca and in Germany during the Seven Years' War, being commended for his skill and personal bravery. Later, as Inspector-General of Cavalry, he improved tactics and soldiers' welfare. Despite speaking no English and having no knowledge of America, he was chosen to command the troops (a third of which were forced to remain in France) sent to America in May 1780. His tact and military bearing overcame his hosts' traditional dislike of Frenchmen, and he succeeded in both repairing the damage caused by his predecessor, d'Estaing, and curbing Lafayette's impetuousness. He served as a politician during the French Revolution, and later as a marshal of France. (Unlike many contemporaries, he escaped the guillotine through the death of Robespierre.)

Maj. Gen. Antoine-Charles du Houx, Baron de Viomenil (1728-1792), was the elder of two brothers serving under Rochambeau as *marechaux-de-camp*[4], both of whom were noted for their good looks, commanding height and fine manners. He joined the Limousin Regiment in 1740 and served in Europe and the Mediterranean, before being appointed *marechal-de-camp* in 1770, and fighting with distinction for the Poles against the Russians. The Baron was Rochambeau's deputy, commanding in his absence during the march to Williamsburg; he was active in the siege, directing the attack on redoubt 9. He died ten years later, of wounds received defending the Tuileries against the Paris mob.

Lieutenant-General de Rochambeau (1725-1807), by C W Peale. The former Inspector-General of Cavalry was a strict disciplinarian, but also showed concern for the welfare of his troops. He had forcefully, but tactfully, refused Lafayette as a liaison officer, believing the latter to be too hot-headed and impetuous, but was prepared to subordinate himself to the professionally inferior Washington for the good of the Allied cause. (Courtesy: Independence National Historical Park, Philadelphia)

Maj. Gen. Francois-Jean de Beauvoir, Chevalier de Chastellux (1734-1788), was third in command of de Rochambeau's corps and, being fluent in English, his unofficial diplomatic representative. He joined the Auvergne Regiment at 13 and was a colonel at 21. After distinguished service in the Seven Years' War, he wrote on military, scientific, philosophical and theatrical matters, and was the first Frenchman to be inoculated against smallpox. Famous for his book, *Travels in North America*, he was reputedly at ease in any company.

Maj. Gen. Charles-Joseph-Hyacinthe du

Houx, Chevalier – or Vicomte – de Viomenil (1734-1827) had, like his older brother, joined the Limousin Regiment at the age of 12. He fought in the War of the Austrian Succession and the Seven Years' War, before becoming a brigadier in 1770 and *marechal-de-camp* in 1780. During the French Revolution, he raised an émigré regiment and commanded a brigade in the Army of Condé before joining the Russian, then Portuguese army.

Major-General Marquis de Chastellux (1734-1788), by C W Peale. As Rochambeau spoke no English, it was left to Chastellux to act as his interpreter at all high-level discussions and negotiations. The Marquis not only fulfilled this post with distinction, but was largely responsible for overcoming the historical distrust of the French felt by many of the senior American officers and politicians. (Courtesy: Independence National Historical Park, Philadelphia)

Maj. Gen. Claude-Anne-Montbleru, Marquis de St Simon (1740-1819), attended the Military School at Strasbourg before joining the Auvergne Regiment. He became colonel of the Touraine Regiment, with which he was serving in the Caribbean when war broke out with Great Britain. Commanding the division sent to Williamsburg with de Grasse, he led the French left during the siege, being slightly wounded while serving in the trenches. In 1790, he left France to serve in the Spanish army (being wounded twice), and later defended Madrid during the siege of 1808. Imprisoned under Napoleon, he was freed on the Bourbon restoration and returned to Spain.

Rear-Admiral Francois Joseph Paul, Comte de Grasse (1722-1788), was a blunt-speaking, talented, six-foot aristocrat. He joined the French navy in 1740, but was captured at Cape Finisterre in 1747, and learned much about the British navy while a captive in England. Following independent commands in the Mediterranean and Caribbean, he commanded a division at Ushant, and squadrons at Savannah and Martinique. Promoted rear-admiral at 60, he returned to America in 1781, and sealed the fate of Cornwallis by forcing Graves's fleet away from Yorktown - the real key to the Allied victory. Captured at the Saints in 1782, further captivity in England resulted in his becoming an intermediary in the peace negotiations. Later tried – and acquitted – for the Saints defeat, his family fled to America when his home and Yorktown relics were destroyed by Revolutionary mobs after his death.

Lieutenant-General de Grasse-Tilly (1722-1788), by J Walker. Despite Washington's logistical and administrative successes in placing the Allied armies at Yorktown, it was de Grasse and his fleet who ensured that Cornwallis was trapped, and prevented his rescue by the Royal Navy. (Courtesy: National Maritime Museum, Greenwich)

Admiral Jacques-Melchior Saint-Laurent, Comte de Barras (*c.*1715-*c.*1800), was technically de Grasse's superior – a fact which did nothing to improve his difficult and unco-operative nature. He had led d'Estaing's squadron in the clumsy attack on Newport in August 1778, and returned to command another French squadron in 1781, when his refusal to co-operate with Washington and Rochambeau, and lack of confidence in the Americans generally, caused problems. He retired in 1783, having captured Monsserrat the previous year.

ACTION AT SPENCER'S TAVERN, 26 JUNE 1781
Following the junction of Lafayette and Wayne, Cornwallis withdrew to Williamsburg, arriving on 25 June, with Lafayette 10 miles away at Bird's tavern. The British rearguard under Simcoe lay halfway between the armies, having been collecting cattle and stores along Chickahominy River. Lafayette sent Colonel John Butler, with 120 riflemen, 100 light infantry, 120 horse and 180 Pennsylvania Continentals to catch Simcoe before he rejoined Cornwallis. At sunrise, 50 dragoons with 50 light infantry riding behind them, surprised Simcoe's pickets at Spencer's Tavern. A brief skirmish saw the American commander, Lt. Col. McPherson unhorsed. Simcoe brought up the main body of his cavalry, forcing back the American horse, until riflemen, and then Butler's reserve appeared. Outnumbered, Simcoe left his wounded in the Tavern, under a flag of truce, and withdrew to Williamsburg, but met Cornwallis' main body and returned to reclaim the battlefield. (Adam Hook)

THE OPPOSING ARMIES

THE BRITISH ARMY

The organisation and command structure of the British Army at the start of the American Revolution was covered in Campaign 37 *Boston 1775*, but tactical improvements rendered Cornwallis's force substantially different from that commanded by Gage six years earlier.

Since the outbreak of war, the line infantry had expanded from 70 to 102 regiments (three more were raised after Yorktown from existing Loyalist units), and three of the seven line infantry units at Yorktown (2/71st, 76th and 80th) were part of that increase. It is indicative of the war's popularity that of the 32 new units, only one – the 71st – was raised before 1778 when the war was solely with the colonists (although existing units were enlarged); but after Saratoga and the entry of France into the conflict, recruiting improved and 12 regiments were raised (six of them in Scotland, including the 76th and 80th).

The single-battalion, ten-company organisation had been retained by the line (the Foot Guards had an *ad hoc* set-up of two four-company battalions, each of three centre companies and a flank company – grenadiers in the 1st Battalion, light infantry in the 2nd Battalion). Officially, line infantry companies had four officers, ten NCOs, two drummers and 100 privates; in practice, a unit's strength depended on its recent service and the frequency of reinforcements. The flank (grenadiers and light) companies of line units were still removed to form 'converged' battalions – a controversial practice which weakened units by removing their best men. When the British abandoned Boston in 1776, they also abandoned the three-rank line for one of two ranks, the rear men covering the gaps in the front rank (called 'loose files'). This 'thin red line' required discipline and coolness when facing denser enemy formations, but a string of victories – often against superior numbers – had proved the efficacy of the system.

Throughout the war, *ésprit de corps* grew as units were brigaded together for long periods: the 23rd and 33rd, for example, came together in 1779, fighting through the Carolinas and Virginia. In terms of experience, the 17th and 23rd had been in America since 1775 (as had the 43rd, which had been in garrison at Newport for three years); the Foot Guards and 71st had arrived in 1776 and served in both northern and southern theatres; the 76th and 80th had arrived in 1779, both over 1,000 strong, but had served only in Virginia (and like many newcomers, were soon reduced by sickness). The light infantry battalions had existed since 1776, but had been re-organised in 1778, when 13 British battalions were sent to the Caribbean; nevertheless, the constituent companies had fought many times together and contained experienced men.

The Royal Regiment of Artillery had also adapted to the new style of warfare and its separate administration – the Board of Ordnance – often referred to by modern historians, made little practical difference in the field. There were two companies at Yorktown, each officially comprising seven officers, six NCOs, 82 gunners and matrosses, and two drummers, though both apparently had fewer officers and more enlisted men. Companies handled all types and sizes of guns – the Yorktown defences had 65 in 14 batteries, including naval 18-pounders.

Finally, a weak troop of the 17th Light Dragoons was attached to Cornwallis's headquarters.

The German Troops

As war approached, the British government realised that the Army was too small, and immediately began negotiating with several minor German rulers for contingents of troops to support the regulars. Much nonsense has been written about 'Hessian mercenaries', but it was common practice in the 18th century for larger countries to augment expensive standing armies with such units. For many minor princelings, such agreements were often the state's only source of income. Ironically, Germans were the one nationality present in numbers in all three armies at Yorktown.

Cornwallis had two German contingents: one from Hesse-Kassel (genuine 'Hessians'); and one from the combined states of Anspach-Bayreuth. Tactically, they used the Prussian system of four divisions of two platoons, so a soldier's administrative (company) and combat (division) officers might be different men. Despite the potential for confusion, lengthy duty in America (and pre-war service) had shown that the system worked – and it would hardly have been retained for so long by the Prussians if it had not. In 1776, Howe had encouraged (though not ordered) the German troops to adopt the British two-rank formation; most contingents did, though they refused to use the 'loose files' believing it to be a tactical weakness. They also seem to have considered the British 'quick march' (in which units moved around the battlefield at a gentle 'trot') as undignified and were equally unwilling to adopt this.

The Hessians comprised two infantry regiments – Erbrpinz (or Prince Hereditaire) and von Bose (previously von Trumbach) – an artillery detachment serving their battalion guns, and a small company of Jäegers. Despite a treaty clause stipulating that Hesse-Kassel units would serve only under their own generals (the only contingent with this agreement), only regimental officers seem to have accompanied Cornwallis. Each regiment was at battalion strength, with (in theory) 18 staff and five companies, each of four officers (the three 'field' officers doubling-up as company commanders, as in British service), 13 NCOs, three drummers and 105 privates. Both regiments had arrived in 1776 with the first Hessian division (which was widely considered the best German unit) and had fought at New York and Philadelphia; the von Bose regiment subsequently served in Virginia.

The Anspach-Bayreuth contingent (two infantry regiments and an artillery company) arrived in America in June 1777 and served together throughout the war, at Philadelphia, New York and Rhode Island, before being sent to Virginia. The first regiment (Col. Voight) was from Anspach, the second (Col. Seybothen) from Bayreuth; both had one grenadier and four musketeer companies, each with a nominal strength of 112 officers and men, plus regimental staff. Although they retained their grenadiers, the contingent's jaeger companies served with the converged Jäeger Corps (formed in 1777 from several German contingents) and so were not at Yorktown. The artillerymen manned the battalion guns.

John Murray, Lord Dunmore (1732-1809) by J Reynolds. Dunmore, along with Josiah Martin the Royal Governor of North Carolina, tried to rally the southern Loyalists. The defeat at Great Bridge (blamed on Dunmore in an anonymous letter to the Government from an officer of the 14th Foot) proved fatal. After his expulsion from Gwynn Island, Dunmore fled to New York and then to Britain. (Courtesy: Scottish National Portrait Gallery, Edinburgh)

The Loyalists

Loyalist units were listed as 'Provincials' on the 'American Establishment' and were not entitled to the same pay, privileges and seniority of rank as the 'Regular (i.e. British and Irish) Establishment'. Two exceptions to this rule were the British Legion (who were taken on to the British Establishment in June 1781) and the Queen's Rangers (1st American Regiment, 1779), both typical of the 'legionary corps' common to this period (supposedly following the writings of Marshal de Saxe, but in North America the phenomenon probably owed more to the lack of mounts).

The British Legion was formed from several Loyalist units and by 1779 were organised as a six-troop British light dragoon regiment. In 1780, four light infantry companies were added, but these were lost at Cowpens. At Yorktown, the Legion apparently reverted to six troops, though shortage of horses may have meant some men served dismounted.

Simcoe's Queen's Rangers had one light, one grenadier, one Highland and eight 'rifle' companies, three troops of light dragoons and one of hussars. It is not clear if all were present at Yorktown – if so, the average strength was barely 20 officers and men. While the Legion had been the more flamboyant of the two corps, recent reverses had damaged its morale and Simcoe had established the Rangers as possibly the most professional and effective light troops on either side.

Little is known about the North Carolina Provincials (or Volunteers) except that a unit of that name served extensively throughout the South with Cornwallis's force, frequently acting as a baggage guard, and may well have been known as the North Carolina Highlanders (who were raised in 1780).

THE ALLIES

Since 1775, the American army had also changed substantially, both in character and organisation[5]. On 1 January 1781, the 'regular army of the United States' underwent its annual re-organisation. Prompted by the expiring of the three-year enlistments of 1777, the number of regiments was reduced, to bring the rest nearer to full strength. That same month, the Pennsylvania Line mutinied over shortages of food, clothing and pay, and the interpretation of their enlistment period. Refusing inducements to defect and handing over British agents to Congress, they marched to Princeton. A review panel discharged over 1,200 men and furloughed another 1,100, which solved their immediate problems but made more for Washington, costing him two brigades (six regiments) of infantry, and prompting more disorder. When the New Jersey Line mutinied

ACTION AT GREEN SPRING FARM, 6 JULY 1781

Leaving Williamsburg and heading for the coast to fulfil Clinton's request for reinforcements, Cornwallis anticipated an attack while the British were crossing the James River and hid his main force in the woods on the north bank. Using false intelligence and a fighting rearguard, he lured Wayne's 1,500-strong advance guard into swampy scrubland, traversed only by a narrow log causeway. As Wayne's skirmishers seized an "aban-doned" gun, the brigades of Yorke and Dundas (about 2,200 men), supported by the Foot Guards,

emerged from the woods. Seeing no other option, Wayne ordered his men to attack and the subsequent musketry duel lasted 15 minutes, before heavy losses forced him to withdraw. Suspecting a trap Lafayette left most of his Continentals in reserve at Green Spring Farm; this reserve, along with nightfall and the poor terrain, prevented Tarleton from destroying Wayne's force, but the Americans still lost 28 dead, 99 wounded and 12 missing, as well as two of their three guns. British losses, including the afternoon's skirmishing, totalled 75, including all three officers of the picket company. (Adam Hook)

(with less justification and more violence), they were surrounded by New Englanders and the two main conspirators were shot by a firing squad composed of the others.

The Continental Army

Under the 1781 re-organisation, the infantry was reduced to 50 regiments, all but one of one battalion; in theory, 'regiment' and 'battalion' were synonymous, but in the field regiments over 160 files (320 men) would split into two battalions. A regiment had one light and eight line companies, each of three officers, nine NCOs, two musicians and 64 privates, a regimental staff of 15, (including a three-man permanent recruiting party) and three field officers. As field officers did not command companies as well, American units were never short of officers and had a pool of experienced senior leaders to command detachments.

Some 49 regiments were allocated to the 'lines' of the 13 states in proportion to the total theoretical manpower of each state. The odd regiment, renamed 'the Canadian Regiment' (formerly Hazen's), had four battalions, each of one light and four line companies, organised as above. Inevitably, the figures were never achieved

in practice – Washington's 'Main Army' was 120 officers and over 10,000 men short of its authorised strengths. When a three-battalion corps of converged light companies was formed under Lafayette, in February 1781, they had only 50 rank-and-file and one of the battalions was completed with line companies from New Jersey. A second 'light corps', formed in March, comprised companies of three officers, five sergeants, two musicians and 50 men chosen from the remaining line companies of various regiments (known as 'provisional' or 'levy' light companies). As with the British, such detachments weakened the donating units, leaving line battalions with establishments of only 100-200 men, and forcing some to amalgamate.

Tactically, the re-organisation gave the American infantry the advantages of a permanent brigade structure with regiments from the same – or neighbouring – states, and a 20 per cent increase in firepower and weight in the charge, using the two-rank formations in von Steuben's drill manual. The ratio of one officer or sergeant per nine enlisted men ensured control and cohesion (unlike the British, Washington was never short of junior officers, as national and local 'politics' ensured an embarrassing over-abundance).

Each of the four artillery regiments was reduced from 12 to ten companies, but gained enlisted men, having six officers, six NCOs, 12 bombardiers and gunners, two musicians and 39 mattrosses each; the regiments also had three field officers (these were also company officers, as technical skills were in short supply) and nine staff.

After successful experiments, the four regiments of light dragoons were converted to 'legionary corps' of mounted and foot untis, as their role invariably required infantry support. Dismounting two of the six troops also saved the cost of 150 horses and equipment. Troops had four officers, eight NCOs, a trumpeter and 60 men (mounted troops also had a farrier). A troop of the 4th Dragoons accompanied Washington's headquarters, along with Armand's Legion, one of two remaining 'Partisan' corps. It was organised as above, but with three mounted and three dismounted troops, and only 50 privates per troop.

The Virginia Militia

The Virginia Militia saw limited action up to 1781, mostly chasing British raiders (with notably little success). However, the units must have contained men who had served together for years – even from before the war – and a few time-expired ex-Continentals. The brigades at Yorktown seem to have served creditably, albeit with substantial French support. Stevens's brigade fled ignominiously at Camden in 1780, but both his and Lawson's brigades fought stubbornly at Guildford. Weedon's brigade had a battalion (Mercer's) which fought in the minor action at Gloucester and was described as 'grenadiers' (probably a euphemism for long-servers).

The French Army

The French Army emerged from the Seven Years' War in such disarray that ministers were given carte blanche to re-form it. The changes included standardisation of training, tactics and equipment; greater financial accountability for officers; military schools; and the ending of the purchase system.

Line infantry regiments were re-organised into one grenadier and one chasseur company, and two four-company battalions of fusiliers. Companies had two platoons, each of two sections, totalling six officers, 16 NCOs, two drummers and 84 men (grenadiers); and six officers, 19 NCOs, two drummers and 144 privates (fusiliers and chasseurs). With a 12-man staff and an auxiliary (training) company, a regiment totalled over 1,800 effectives on paper, but at Yorktown, St Simon's units averaged only 1,000, and those from Newport just 900 (albeit after Rochambeau had lent 700 men to de Barras's fleet and left 400 more to guard the base; in addition, many men had fallen sick on the march south). With the exception of Touraine, the regiments were paired into brigades, named after the senior unit.

The infantry used the 'Prussian order', manoeuvring and firing in three ranks, but retained the traditional attack column. An army assembled in 1778 to invade England had compared the two systems, and the linear tactics championed by de Rochambeau had triumphed, prompting his appointment. The French were intrigued by the new two-rank British formation and were eager to take it on, believing that their three-rank line would punch through it. (Though British troops from America had already beaten a larger French force on St Lucia in 1779.)

The Royal-Artillerie comprised seven regiments, each of 20 companies (four of bombardiers, two of sappers and the remainder gunners), organised either into two ten-company battalions, or five four-company brigades. Companies had four officers and 71 NCOs and men; the guns and equipment were of the Gribeauval system, with 4-, 8- and 12-pdr. field guns, and 18- or 24-pdr. siege guns. A battalion of the Auxonne Regiment and companies of the Metz Regiment supported Rochambeau in America.

The Corps Royal de l'Infanterie de la Marine comprised 100 infantry companies and three bombardier companies to provide marine detachments and supervise naval gunnery. The infantry companies had three officers, 19 NCOs, three drummers and 96 fusiliers; the bombardiers had four officers, seven NCOs, 12 artificers, 50 bombardiers and a drummer. De Grasse landed some 800 marines to assist in the siege of Gloucester Point.

In 1778, it was decided to form eight legions of Volontaires étranger de la Marine, comprising Germans, Poles, Hungarians and Irishmen, for overseas service. Each of the three legions actually raised consisted of four infantry companies (one grenadier, one chasseur, two fusilier) of 75 men, and individual companies of gunners, workmen and hussars. The corps also had a compagnie générale of hussars as headquarters troops.

The Duc de Lauzun was appointed brigadier of the corps and also commanded the 2 ème Legion (renamed Lauzun's Legion), which formed part of Rochambeau's corps. A shortage of transports forced Lauzun to leave many of his men behind, but he was still able to take 250 infantry in four companies, a small detachment of 60 gunners, and two hussar squadrons of 150 men each (his own and the compagnie générale). Half the cavalry (probably Lauzun's own squadron, which may have contained a number of Poles) appear to have been armed with lances. A small unit of 50 'hussars' accompanied St Simon's headquarters; these may well have been from the 1ère Legion which was stationed the West Indies.

CORNWALLIS'S FORCES AT GREEN SPRING FARM, 6 JULY 1781

Commanding: Lt.Gen. Cornwallis

Unit strength	
17th Light Dragoons	24
British Legion	207*
Lt. Col. Yorke	
1st Light Infantry	494*
2nd Light Infantry	374*
Brigade of Guards	538*
23rd Foot	225
33rd Foot	231
Lt. Col. Dundas	
Royal Artillery (two 6-pdrs.)	40*
43rd Foot	287*
76th Foot	522*
80th Foot	520*
CAMP GUARD (north bank)	
2/71st Foot	227
82nd Foot, Light Coy.	37
von Bose	341
Jaegers	45
BAGGAGE GUARD *Lt. Col. Simcoe* (south bank)	
Queen's Rangers Cavalry	120
Queen's Rangers Infantry	240
North Carolina Loyalists	140

(Only units marked * were engaged)

LAFAYETTE'S FORCES AT GREEN SPRING FARM, 6 JULY 1781

Commanding: Maj.Gen. Lafayette

Brig. Gen. Wayne

Unit strength	
Advance Guard (Light Infantry)	60*(Galvan)
1st Pennsylvania Line	300*
2nd Pennsylvania Line	300*
3rd Pennsylvania Line	300*
Gimat's Light Battalion (part)	200*(Wyllys)
Virginia Rifle Companies	200*(Call, Willis)
Armand's Legion Cavalry	60*
1st Continental Dragoons	100*
Continental Artillery (three 4-pdrs.) (2 Pennsylvania, 1 Massachusetts)	50*
RESERVE: *Lt. Col. Gimat*	
Gimat's Light Battalion (part)	190 (Gimat)
Vose's Light Battalion	370
Barber's Light Battalion	380
REARGUARD: *Maj. Gen. von Steuben* (Bird's Tavern)	
Virginia Continentals (Febiger)	450
Virginia Militia Brigade (Stevens)	750
Virginia Militia Brigade (Lawson)	750
Virginia Militia Riflemen (Campbell)	600

(Only units marked * were engaged)

ARBUTHNOT'S FORCES OFF CAPE HENRY, 16 MARCH 1781

Commanding: Mariot Arbuthnot, Vice-Admiral of the White
Thomas Graves, Rear-Admiral of the Blue

Vessel	Guns
America	64
Bedford	64
Adamant	50
London (Graves)	90
Royal Oak (Arbuthnot)	74
Prudent	64
Europe	64
Robust	64
Iris	32
Pearl	32
Guadeloupe	28

DESTOUCHES' FORCES OFF CAPE HENRY, 16 MARCH 1781

Commanding: Chevalier Destouches
Maj. Gen. Baron de Viomenil, 1,200 infantry

Vessel	Guns
Neptune	74
Bourgogne (Destouches)	74
Conquérant	74
Provence	64
Ardent	64
Jason	64
Eveille	64
Romulus	44
Hermione	36
Gentille	32
Fantasque	64

GRAVES' FORCES OFF THE CAPES, 5 SEPTEMBER 1781

Commanding: Thomas Graves, Rear-Admiral of the Red
Sir Samuel Hood, Rear-Admiral of the Blue
Sir Francis Drake, Rear-Admiral of the Blue

Vessel	Guns
Alfred	74
Belligueux	64
Invincible	74
Barfleur (Hood)	98
Monarch	74
Centaur	74
America	64
Resolution	74
Bedford	74
London (Graves)	90
Royal Oak	74
Montagu	74
Europe	64
Terrible	74
Ajax	74
Princessa (Drake)	70
Alcide	74
Intrepid	64
Shrewsbury	74
Adamant	50
La Fortunee	38
La Nymphe	36
Santa Monica	32
Richmond	32
Solebay	28
Sybil	28
Salamander (Fireship)	8

DE GRASSE'S FORCES OFF THE CAPES, 5 SEPTEMBER 1781

Commanding: Rear-Admiral Francois, Comte de Grasse

Vessel	Guns
Pluton	74
Marseilles	74
Bourgogne	74
Diademe	74
Refleche	64
Auguste	80
Saint-Esprit	80
Canton	64
Cesar	74
Destin	74
Ville de Paris (Grasse)	110
Victoire	74
Sceptre	74
Northumberland	74
Palmier	74
Solitaire	64
Citoyen	74
Scipione	74
Hercule	74
Magnanime	74
Languedoc	80
Zele	74
Hector	74
Souverain	74
Andromaque	32
Rayeuse	32
Surveillante	16
Concorde	36
Gentille	32
Diligente	26
Aigrette	26

The vessels *Glorieux* (74), *Triton* (64), *Vaillant* (64) and *Experiment* (50) were left to guard the entrances to the York and James rivers.

CORNWALLIS'S FORCES AT YORKTOWN, 1 SEPTEMBER 1781

(These strengths are derived from the American returns of prisoners on 19 October, as well as the figures for dead and missing given by Tarleton.)

Commanding: Lt. Gen. Charles, Earl Cornwallis

HEADQUARTERS:

Staff	(23 officers, 69 other ranks)
17th Light Dragoons	(2, 22)
Marines	(about 800)

ARTILLERY:

Capt. George Rochfort	
Royal Regiment of Artillery	(11, 226)
(plus detachments of sailors manning guns from scuttled ships)	

BRITISH INFANTRY:

Brigade of Foot Guards - Brig. Gen. Charles O'Hara	
Two battalions	(20, 518)

Light Infantry Brigade - Lt. Col. Robert Abercrombie (38th Foot)

1st Battalion	(16, 429)
(Light companies of the 4th, 15th, 17th, 23rd, 27th, 33rd and 38th Foot)	
2nd Battalion	(16, 326)
(Light companies of the 37th, 40th, 43rd, 45th, 49th, 55th, 63rd and 71st Foot)	
82nd Foot	(2, 37)

First Brigade - Lt. Col. John Yorke (22nd Foot)

17th Foot	(18, 228)
23rd Foot	(13, 231)
33rd Foot	(13, 263)
71st Foot, 2nd Bn.	(22, 299)

Second Brigade - Lt. Col. Thomas Dundas (80th Foot)

43rd Foot	(15, 366)
76th Foot	(30, 691) *
80th Foot	(32, 668) *

GERMAN INFANTRY:

Anspach-Bayreuth Contingent – *Col. August von Voigt*

1st Regt. - von Voigt:	(26, 519) +
2nd Regt. - von Seybothen:	(24, 508) +
Artillery company	(1, 43 serving four 3-pdrs.)

Hesse-Kassel Contingent - *Lt. Col. Matthew von Fuchs*

Erb Prinz [Prince Hereditaire] Regt.	(18, 498)
von Bose Regt.	(13, 364)
Jaeger Coy.	(5, 67)
Artillery Coy.	(2, 49 serving four 4-pdrs.)

LOYALISTS:

Queen's Rangers	(43, 277)
British Legion	(25, 216)
North Carolina Volunteers	(23, 121)
Detachments	(12, 10)
Pioneers	(5, 37)

* These units still had their grenadier and light companies attached.

\+ These units still had their grenadier companies attached.

(NB: The units that served at Gloucester Point have not been indicated, as the make-up of that garrison varied during the siege.)

WASHINGTON'S FORCES AT YORKTOWN, 28 SEPTEMBER 1781

THE AMERICANS

Commander-in-chief: Gen. George Washington

Unit Strength

HEADQUARTERS:

4th Continental Dragoons	60
Armand's Legion	40

ARTILLERY:

Brig.Gen. Henry Knox	
1st Continental Artillery (1 coy.)	25
2nd Continental Artillery (9 coys.)	225
4th Continental Artillery (3 coys.)	60
Sappers & Miners (4 coys.)	110

INFANTRY:

Light Division - *Maj.Gen. Marquis de Lafayette*

1st Brigade: *Brig.Gen.. Peter Muhlenberg*

Col. Vose's Bn.	(21, 288)*
(8 Massachusetts light companies)+	
Lt.Col. Gimat's Bn.	(17, 283)
(5 Connecticut, 2 Massachusetts, 1 Rhode Island light companies)	
Lt.Col. Barber's Bn.	(21, 336)
(2 New Hampshire, 2 New Jersey, 1 Canadian light companies; 3 New Jersey line companies)	

2nd Brigade: Brig.Gen. Moses Hazen

Lt.Col. Scammell's Bn.	(24, 354)

(2 New Hampshire, 3 Massachusetts, 3 Connecticut light companies)

Lt. Col. Hamilton's Bn.	(16, 231)

(2 New York light companies; 2 New York, 2 Connecticut provisional light companies)

Hazen's Canadian Regt.	(21,246)

Second Division - *Maj. Gen. Benjamin Lincoln*

1st Brigade: *Brig. Gen. James Clinton*

1st New York	(24, 367)
2nd New York	(23, 398)

2nd Brigade: *Col. Elias Dayton*

1st New Jersey	(15, 150)
2nd New Jersey	(18, 141)
Rhode Island	(25, 334)

Third Division - *Maj. Gen. Baron von Steuben*

1st Brigade: *Brig. Gen.. Anthony Wayne*

1st Pennsylvania Bn.	(19, 267)
2nd Pennsylvania Bn.	(21, 289)
3rd Virginia	(27, 348)

2nd Brigade: *Brig. Gen. Mordecai Gist*

3rd Maryland	(27, 404)
4th Maryland	(450)

Virginia Militia: *General Thomas Nelson*

1st Brigade: *Brig. Gen.George Weedon*	1,500 x
2nd Brigade: *Brig. Gen.Robert Lawson*	750
3rd Brigade: *Brig. Gen.Edward Stevens*	750
Dabney's State Legion	(7, 193)

* The figures in brackets are for officers and men present and fit for duty; those sick or serving 'on detachment' are not included.

+ The term 'light company' refers to those units that were an integral part of the regular establishment of each Continental regiment; the term 'provisional light company' refers to those units formed by drafting men from the centre companies of Continental regiments whose own light companies had already been detached.

x This unit served at Gloucester Point.

THE FRENCH

Commanding: Lt-Gen. Comte de Rochambeau (Yorktown)

ARTILLERY:

Lt. Col. Comte d'Aboville

Auxonne Regt. (1 bn.)	600
Metz Regt. (1 coy.)	70

INFANTRY*:*

Maj. Gen. Baron de Viomenil's Division

Brigade Bourbonnois: *Col. Marquis de Laval*

Bourbonnois Regt. (2 bns.)	900
Royal Deux-Ponts Regt. (2 bns.)	900

Maj. Gen. Vicomte de Viomenil's Division

Brigade Soissonois: *Col. Marquis de St Maime*

Soissonois Regt. (2 bns.)	900
Saintonge Regt. (2 bns.)	900

*Maj. Gen. Marquis de St Simon's Division**

Brigade Agenois: *Col. Marquis d'Audechamp*

Agenois Regt. (2 bns.)	1,000
Gatinois Regt. (2 bns.)	1,000

Brigade Touraine: *Col. Vicomte de Pondeux*

Touraine Regt. (2 bns.)	1,000

DETACHMENT:

Brig. Gen. Marquis de Choisy (Gloucester)

Marines	800
Lauzun's Legion	600

(2 squadrons of hussars from the compagnie générale & 2 ème Legion; 4 companies of infantry and detachment of gunners, 2 ème Legion)

* Included 50 hussars, probably from 1ère Volontaires Etranger de la Marine; 100 "Volontaires de St. Simon" a light infantry unit, probably composed of colonial troops; and a detachment from the Belzunce Dragoons, which accompanied his headquaters.

CORNWALLIS VERSUS LAFAYETTE

The British take the war into Virginia and attempt to catch and destroy Lafayette and his force of Continentals

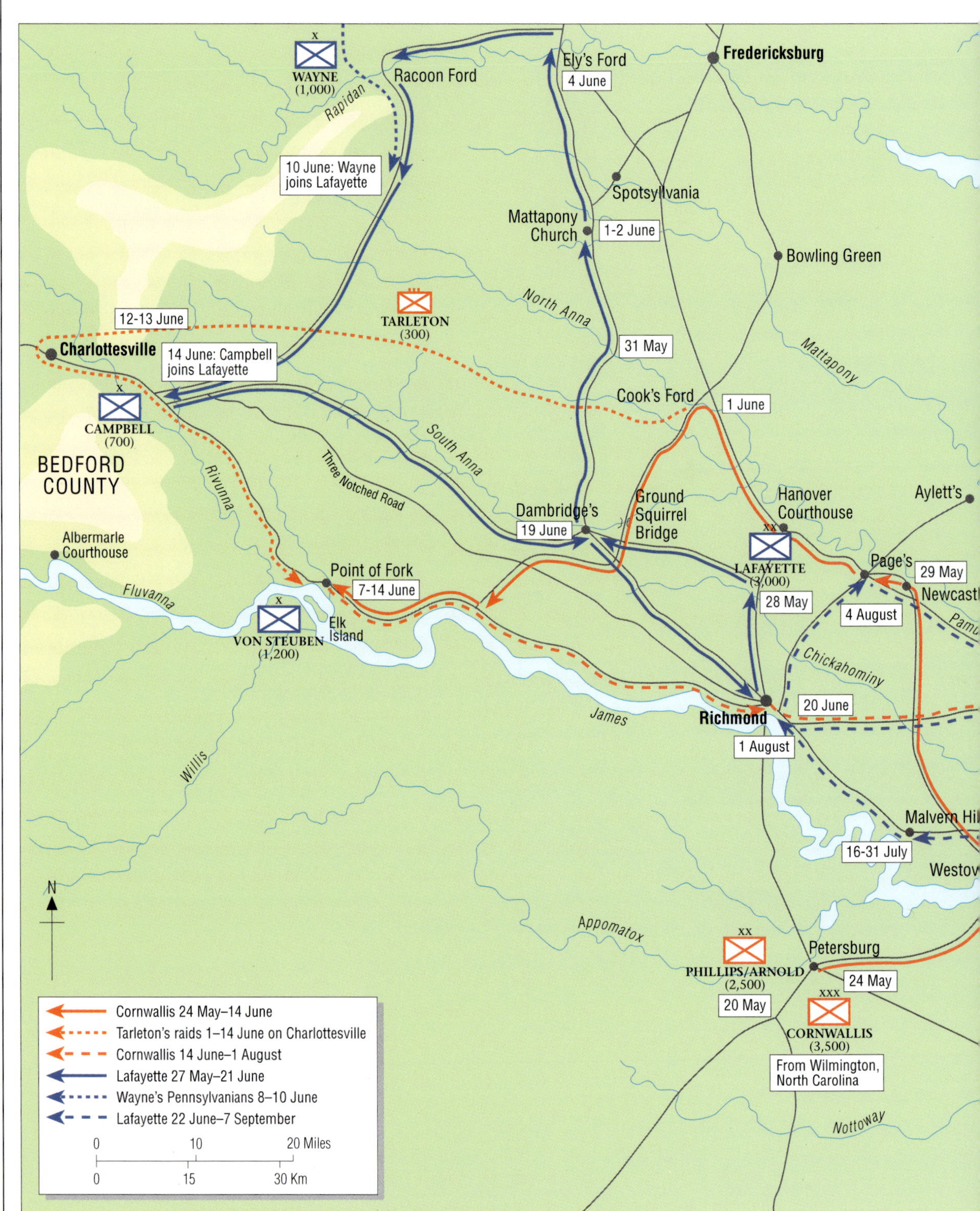

THE CAMPAIGN IN VIRGINIA 1781

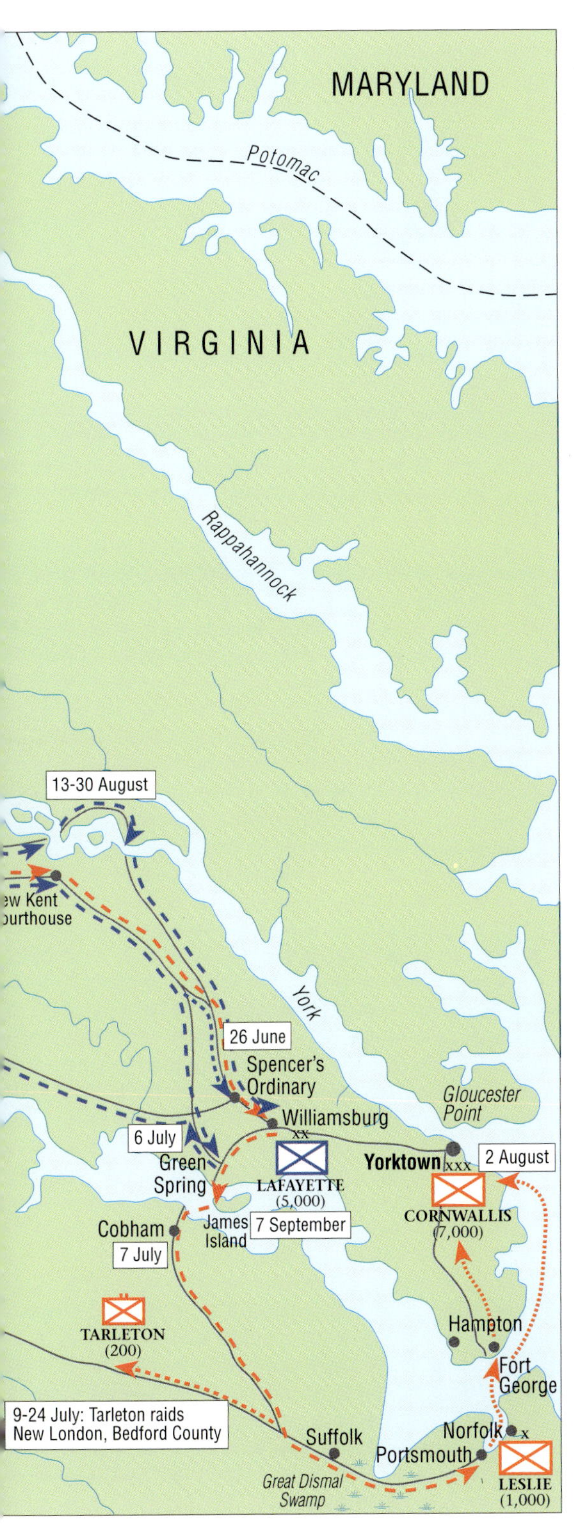

On 25 April, Cornwallis left Wilmington with 1,500 fit men. Halting at Halifax, near the Roanoke River, he learned that Greene had ignored the bait and returned to South Carolina to help the partisans mop up isolated British garrisons. When, on 12 May, Cornwallis was informed that Rawdon had beaten Greene at Hobkirk's Hill, he assumed that it was now safe to enter Virginia and join Phillips. Only when it was too late did he discover that Rawdon, despite his victory, had been forced to abandon Camden and three other British posts.

Criss-crossing the rivers Neuse and Tar, Cornwallis sent Lt.Col. Banastre Tarleton and his British Legion cavalry ahead to forage, but the dry weather and hostile countryside frustrated even his efforts. When the Earl arrived at Petersburg on 20 May, his army was once again weakened by malnutrition and heat exhaustion; to make matters worse, his friend Phillips had died of typhoid fever five days before, leaving Arnold in command.

Cornwallis found Phillips's instructions from Clinton to fortify Portsmouth – or any other suitable place – as a naval base. He also found a report from Lt.Col. von Fuchs, commanding at Portsmouth, stating that merely maintaining the existing light defences required 400 men, and that the heat and severity of the work was encouraging desertion and sickness. Cornwallis was only too well aware of the latter problem, as barely 5,000 of his 7,000 men were fit for duty. Sending Leslie to take over at Portsmouth, Cornwallis organised raids to destroy enemy stores and force Lafayette (commanding the only Continentals in Virginia) away from Richmond. He told Clinton he would move his base to Williamsburg, which had a healthier climate and was close to Yorktown, the town widely felt to be the most suitable site for the naval base.

CORNWALLIS AGAINST LAFAYETTE

Lafayette had arrived in Richmond at the end of April with 3,000 men, tasked with capturing Arnold and preventing British raids. When Cornwallis crossed the James River, he withdrew through Hannover,

shadowing his opponent while also moving towards a brigade of Pennsylvanians marching through Maryland under Brig. Gen. Anthony Wayne Cornwallis, knowing he had a month's grace until Clinton's reply, recognised the futility of chasing Lafayette, particularly after his experiences with Greene, and he saw little chance that Clinton would allow him to pursue a full-blooded campaign. However, Lafayette's withdrawal had exposed the south and west of Virginia to raiding parties and Cornwallis had two highly capable men to lead them.

First, he ordered Tarleton to take 180 cavalry and 70 mounted infantry and 'disturb' the Virginia Assembly at Charlottesville. On 4 June, Tarleton charged into the town, capturing several delegates (but missing Jefferson and his family by minutes) and destroying all the stores he could find.

Meanwhile, Simcoe was ordered to Point of Fork, at the junction of the rivers Rivanna and Fluvanna, to destroy stores and, if possible, the 2-300 militia von Steuben had gathered. Taking every fit man of the Queen's Rangers (about 200 infantry – 50 of them barefoot – and 100 cavalry), the 2/71st Foot and a 3-pdr., Simcoe headed off, imprisoning every man he met on the road.

Hearing that von Steuben was transporting stores across the Fluvanna, Simcoe's men captured some enemy dragoons, exchanged uniforms and galloped to a nearby house to capture the Baron (who narrowly just evaded them). Discovering that von Steuben actually had over 1,000 men, Simcoe ordered the red-coated 71st, the women and the baggage, to camp in nearby woods to suggest that the main British army had arrived. The rest of his troops occupied a hill overlooking the river and commenced a one-round bombardment with their 3-pounder. By the next morning, the Americans had disappeared, abandoning 2,500 stand of arms, as well as powder, wagons, tools and ten pieces of ordnance which Cornwallis quickly absorbed into his own artillery park on 7 June.

On 10 June, Wayne's command joined Lafayette's command, half of which now consisted of Continentals, while the remainder comprised militia who had fought in the South at Guildford and King's Mountain. Cornwallis decided to return down the James River to Williamsburg, relying on his more numerous cavalry to prevent surprises. Lafayette tried to lure him back by dividing his force, but by then Cornwallis was more interested in Clinton's plans for his army.

Lieutenant-Colonel Banastre Tarleton (1754-1833), by J Reynolds. Tarleton (1754-1833) joined the Army in 1775 and volunteered for America, serving in the 16th Light Dragoons and the 79th Foot, before leading the British Legion at Monmouth. His ruthlessness in the South made his name synonymous with cruelty and despite several flamboyant successes, his defeat at Cowpens was seen as a comeuppance by colleagues and opponents alike. After an unsuccessful post-war career in politics, he returned to the Army during the French Revolution, but held no active commands and eventually retired to private life.(Courtesy: National Gallery, London)

On 25 June, he arrived in Williamsburg, with Lafayette ten miles behind. Lafayette decided to test the British rearguard, sending Colonel Butler's dragoons and light infantry to Spencer's Ordinary (or Tavern), midway between the two armies. Running into Simcoe's Rangers and some jäegers (who had been busy collecting cattle and stores on the Chickahominy River)), heavy fighting ensued, with the British withdrawing towards Williamsburg. Though Cornwallis arrived with reinforcements, allowing Simcoe to reclaim the field, the action had shown the quality of Lafayette's men. The British had 33 casualties (Lafayette claimed 160), and the Americans slightly more, including 31 prisoners.

The next day, Cornwallis received two letters from Clinton, who was clearly unhappy with the march into Virginia, especially since learning that Washington and Rochambeau had met in May to discuss future combined operations. Assuming (probably correctly, at that time) that their most likely objective was New York, and would undoubtedly involve the French fleet that had been entering American waters from the Caribbean each summer since 1778, he asked Cornwallis to send back immediately six regiments of infantry, all the mounted troops and whatever artillery could be spared. The rest of his force was to be used to carry out Clinton's original plan to establish a naval base in the Chesapeake.

Disenchanted as he was with Clinton's indirectness and his obsession with a naval base in Chesapeake Bay, Cornwallis reconnoitred the York Peninsula down to Old Point Comfort and Hampton Roads, with Simcoe on 28 June. None of the proposed sites appeared very suitable for his purpose, so Cornwallis returned to Williamsburg, determined to fulfil at least part of his orders by withdrawing to Portsmouth. Once there, he would send to New York as many men as could fit on the available transports, with the rest following when more ships arrived, he would then decide if Portsmouth could be defended adequately with what remained.

ACTION AT GLOUCESTER POINT, 3 OCTOBER 1781

By 2 October, the Allies had trapped Cornwallis, but had not yet invested Gloucester, so Cornwallis sent Tarleton across with the mounted troops to find food. The next day, as a foraging party was returning to Gloucester, Tarleton observed French cavalry, under the Duc de Lauzun, pursuing them. In order to allow the wagons to escape, Tarleton charged the leading group of lancers as they emerged from a long narrow lane. The two leaders were about to engage in single combat when Tarleton was dismounted by a wounded horse and only the arrival of his men prevented

Lauzun capturing him. Further charges failed to break Lauzun's cavalry and with french infantry arriving to his front, and a veteran American militia unit and more French hussars approaching his right, Tarleton withdrew. The action was the largest cavalry fight of the war – and highly colourful, with Lauzun's men in sky blue and yellow and Tarleton's in either green coats or the white smocks they wore in the hotter southern regions. Casualties were light – three Frenchmen dead and 16 wounded; 12 dead or captured on the British side – the only infantry casualty was a British officer killed by the militia. (Adam Hook)

THE ACTION AT GREEN SPRING FARM

On 4 July, Cornwallis prepared to cross the James River at a ferry near Jamestown Island. Anticipating an attack during the two days needed to ferry the baggage across, he prepared a trap for Lafayette (who had boasted that Cornwallis was running away from him). The British position was extremely strong, covered by several small ponds on the right, a morass on the left, and dense woods along the front. The only approach was along a causeway that ran from the river to Green Spring Farm, a mile away, across a lightly wooded swamp

Lafayette had reached Chickahominy Church (Norrell's Mills) by 5 July, with the advance guard under Wayne closing on the British, unaware that Cornwallis had hidden his main force (apart from the Queen's Rangers and some Loyalist infantry) on the north bank of the river. As Wayne neared, two 'deserters' convinced him that only their units stood in front of him, whereupon he rushed forward to Green Spring Farm. There, he was joined by Lafayette, who ordered up the

Brigadier-General Anthony Wayne (1745-1796), by J Sharples. When war broke out, Wayne, a tanner with experience as a surveyor and land agent, became a Colonel. He took part in the retreat from Canada and briefly commanded Ticonderoga (where he learned how to handle a mutiny). He led the Pennsylvania Line at Brandywine, Germantown and Monmouth and captured Stony Point in 1779. After quelling the mutiny of Pennsylvania troops in early 1781, he led a brigade under Lafayette in Virginia. In 1783 he left the army, farmed in Georgia, and dabbled in politics. In 1792 he successfully took over the demoralised army fighting the native tribes in the north-west, earning the nickname 'Mad Anthony'. (Courtesy: Independence National Historical Park, Philadelphia)

Light Infantry and Pennsylvanian brigades to inflict a crushing defeat on the British. Meanwhile, Wayne sent forward two bodies of riflemen, supported by some light infantry and his cavalry contingent, his sole battalion of Pennsylvanians forming a reserve.

Wayne's men spent the afternoon skirmishing with Tarleton's Legion cavalry and a picket company of regular infantry, who had strict orders to add weight to the ruse by contesting every yard of ground. At about 5:00pm, the reinforcements ordered up by Lafayette arrived, but the Frenchman had become suspicious and sent forward only the Pennsylvanians, holding the Light Infantry at the farm. He then rode down to the river, where a tongue of land allowed him to observe Cornwallis's true strength.

As Lafayette galloped back to warn Wayne, the American skirmish line emerged from the wooded swamp and the light infantry detachment ran forward to seize an 'abandoned' gun beside the causeway - the signal for the British to burst from the woods. Forming rapidly into lines, their sudden appearance stunned Wayne's command and his skirmishers fell back onto his left. Clearly outflanked on both sides, Wayne saw no hope of defending and, forming his Continentals into line, advanced. For 15 minutes, the two sides traded volleys at 70 yards and less, until the British Light Infantry brushed aside the American left and threatened to surround the centre.

Gradually, Wayne's line dissolved: two of his three guns lost all their horses and had to be abandoned, and every field officer was dismounted. Lafayette, who had two horses shot dead under him, rode back to Green Spring Farm and arranged his reserve to cover the retreat. As Wayne's command fled, only the swampy ground and the fast-failing light saved them from destruction by Tarleton's cavalry (who blamed the failure to pursue on Cornwallis). During the night, Lafayette pulled back to Chickahominy Church to join Lawson's militia and von Steuben's division which had advanced 12 miles from Bird's Tavern. Tarleton's cavalry and mounted infantry located them the next morning, but withdrew reluctantly, without engaging.

Despite Tarleton's protestations, Cornwallis could not have profitably pursued Lafayette, whose hitherto uncommitted units were as fresh as the British were weary. The best British scouts, and the baggage, were on the far side of the river, and – even had Lafayette desired it – a major battle, though probably successful for the British, would have incurred losses among the men earmarked to reinforce Clinton. As it was, they had suffered 75 casualties, including five officers wounded – a commodity already in dangerously short supply. The Americans lost over 150 dead, wounded and missing, including 100 Pennsylvanians. Once again, however, an American force had been decisively beaten, but (albeit through no skill of its own) had avoided total destruction.

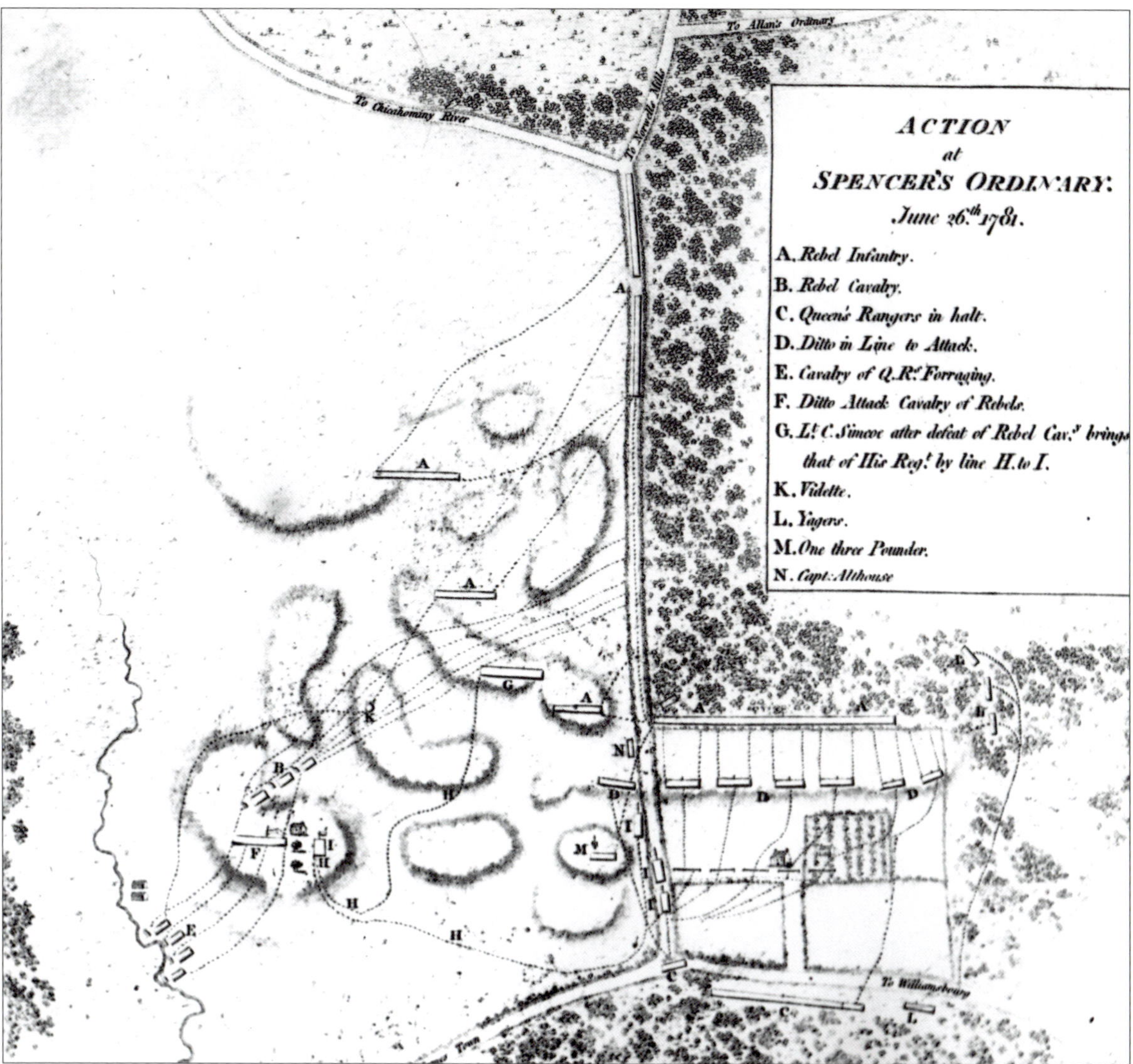

Action at Spencer's Ordinary, 26 June 1781. This map, drawn for Simcoe's memoirs, gives misleading clarity to the highly confused action around Spencer's Tavern. Top left; McPherson's mixed group surprises the pickets of the Queen's Rangers, and is then counter-attacked by Simcoe's cavalry, which had been watering at the creek (bottom left). The cavalry then joined the infantry, stationed to the right of the road to attack Butler's reserve, with the jäegers turning the American left (bottom right). (Courtesy: Colonial Williamsburg)

Having completed the crossing of the James River, the British headed for Suffolk. On 9 July, Tarleton set off for south-western Virginia, to destroy stores which, it transpired, had already been sent to Greene. He arrived back at Suffolk on 24 July, having reached New London at the foot of the Blue Ridge Mountains (a 400-mile round trip), but having achieved little beyond exhausting his men and horses.

Cornwallis himself arrived at Suffolk on 12 July. Here he received a letter from Clinton apparently playing down the threat to New York and introducing a new plan for Cornwallis to march into Pennsylvania (and establish a base in Chesapeake Bay), while Clinton attacked either Philadelphia or Newport. Keeping ten transports for his remaining men and horses, Cornwallis sent most of his men to Portsmouth; as they were embarking for Philadelphia on 20 July, another letter arrived from Clinton, insisting that he immediately disembark and, with his whole force, establish a base at Old Point Comfort to control Hampton Roads. Although Cornwallis had pointed out before that raids into Chesapeake Bay would be more effectively undertaken from New York, than from a

PHASE 2 **15.00 - 17.00 Hrs. Driving back the British pickets, Wayne crosses the causeway through wooded marshes confident of catching Cornwallis's rearguard before it can cross the James River. As he advances he is joined by reinforcements called up by Lafayette**

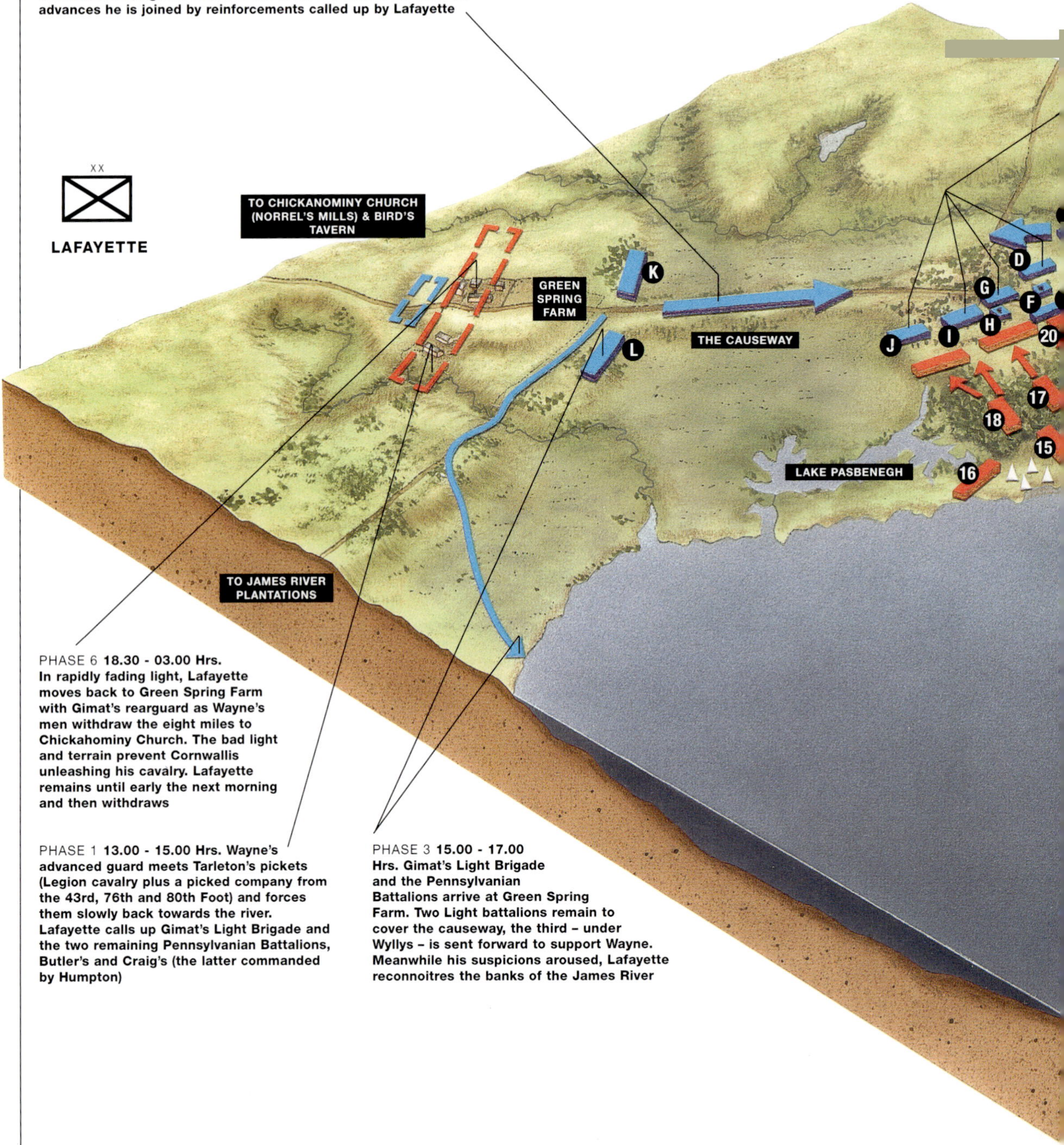

XX

LAFAYETTE

TO CHICKANOMINY CHURCH (NORREL'S MILLS) & BIRD'S TAVERN

GREEN SPRING FARM

K

L

THE CAUSEWAY

D

G

F

H

I

J

20

17

18

15

16

LAKE PASBENEGH

TO JAMES RIVER PLANTATIONS

PHASE 6 **18.30 - 03.00 Hrs.**
In rapidly fading light, Lafayette moves back to Green Spring Farm with Gimat's rearguard as Wayne's men withdraw the eight miles to Chickahominy Church. The bad light and terrain prevent Cornwallis unleashing his cavalry. Lafayette remains until early the next morning and then withdraws

PHASE 1 **13.00 - 15.00 Hrs. Wayne's advanced guard meets Tarleton's pickets (Legion cavalry plus a picked company from the 43rd, 76th and 80th Foot) and forces them slowly back towards the river. Lafayette calls up Gimat's Light Brigade and the two remaining Pennsylvanian Battalions, Butler's and Craig's (the latter commanded by Humpton)**

PHASE 3 **15.00 - 17.00**
Hrs. Gimat's Light Brigade and the Pennsylvanian Battalions arrive at Green Spring Farm. Two Light battalions remain to cover the causeway, the third – under Wyllys – is sent forward to support Wayne. Meanwhile his suspicions aroused, Lafayette reconnoitres the banks of the James River

ENGAGEMENT AT GREEN SPRING
6 JULY 1781

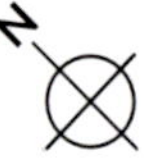

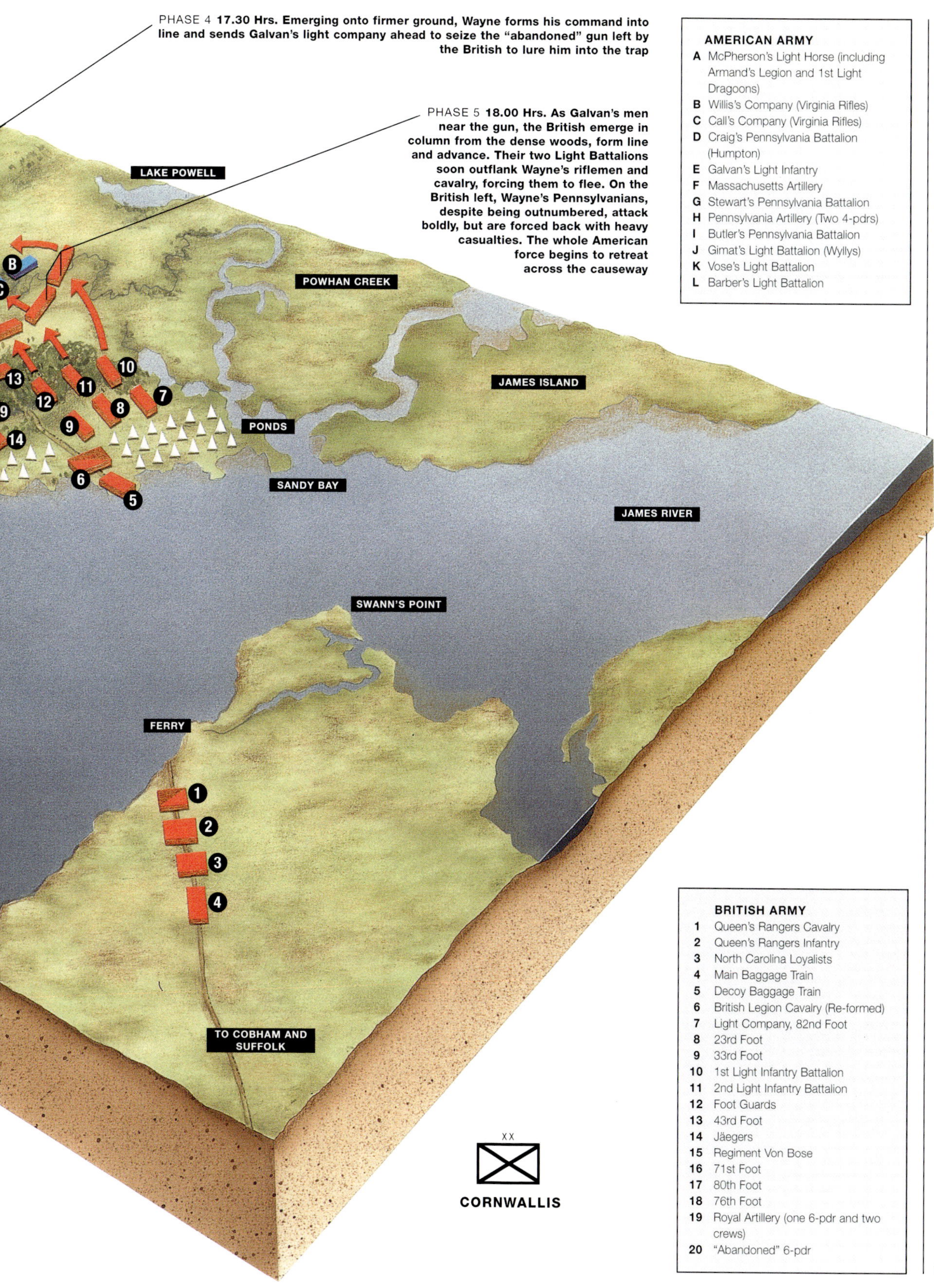

AMERICAN ARMY

- **A** McPherson's Light Horse (including Armand's Legion and 1st Light Dragoons)
- **B** Willis's Company (Virginia Rifles)
- **C** Call's Company (Virginia Rifles)
- **D** Craig's Pennsylvania Battalion (Humpton)
- **E** Galvan's Light Infantry
- **F** Massachusetts Artillery
- **G** Stewart's Pennsylvania Battalion
- **H** Pennsylvania Artillery (Two 4-pdrs)
- **I** Butler's Pennsylvania Battalion
- **J** Gimat's Light Battalion (Wyllys)
- **K** Vose's Light Battalion
- **L** Barber's Light Battalion

BRITISH ARMY

- **1** Queen's Rangers Cavalry
- **2** Queen's Rangers Infantry
- **3** North Carolina Loyalists
- **4** Main Baggage Train
- **5** Decoy Baggage Train
- **6** British Legion Cavalry (Re-formed)
- **7** Light Company, 82nd Foot
- **8** 23rd Foot
- **9** 33rd Foot
- **10** 1st Light Infantry Battalion
- **11** 2nd Light Infantry Battalion
- **12** Foot Guards
- **13** 43rd Foot
- **14** Jäegers
- **15** Regiment Von Bose
- **16** 71st Foot
- **17** 80th Foot
- **18** 76th Foot
- **19** Royal Artillery (one 6-pdr and two crews)
- **20** "Abandoned" 6-pdr

tiny, sweltering post vulnerable to local assault (and any overwhelming French fleet that happened to be passing), he proceeded to fulfil this rare direct order.

ABOVE **A view of Yorktown. This etching shows an almost plan-view of Yorktown and the area around it during the siege, including the British defensive line, and the York River and Gloucester Point. The two creeks – Yorktown and Wormley – which cut into the peninsula and dictated the Allies' line of approach, can be seen clearly. (Courtesy: Anne S K Brown Collection, Providence)**

Unfortunately, his chief engineer, Lt. Sutherland, found Old Point Comfort totally unsuitable for fortifying, while the naval officers present unanimously disapproved of it as an anchorage. Having examined it himself, Cornwallis agreed and decided that, if Clinton really wanted such a post, the most suitable from a naval viewpoint was Yorktown, but the lie of the land around the latter meant that exceptionally strong fortifications would be required.

As his men sailed up-river to Yorktown, where they disembarked on 2 August, Cornwallis sent Leslie to Charleston to replace Rawdon (who had fallen ill), leaving O'Hara in charge at Portsmouth with orders to destroy the defences and then move north to re-join Cornwallis. Working his men and hundreds of runaway slaves who had joined him to the limit, Cornwallis strove to fortify the former tobacco port at the junction of the York and James rivers with Chesapeake Bay.

THE ALLIES MOVE SOUTH

Four hundred miles away, Washington could do little to assist in the South, and saw no prospect of an opening in the North. Worse, the stalemate was creating apathy and discouraging recruitment, leaving the army short of men, clothing, equipment, food and pay. On 22 May, he had met Rochambeau at Wethersfield, where they had discussed either reinforcing the South, where the enemy were at their strongest in relation to American forces (though Cornwallis's presence in Virginia was not yet known) by weakening the North (where the British were at their weakest since 1775), or awaiting the arrival of the French fleet and mounting a combined attack on New York. The latter offered a more immediate prospect of success, as the cautious Clinton would undoubtedly recall troops from the South. What Washington needed most, though, was detailed information on French naval movements, which Rochambeau would not – or could not – provide.

The conference ended without any firm decision, beyond Rochambeau agreeing to join the Americans at Peeskill. His corps duly left Newport on 9 June and arrived at White Plains on 6 July, five days after the Duc de Lauzun and his Legion had participated in a recon-

Skirmishes at Blandford and Petersburg, 25 April 1781. On 24 April, Phillips's marched towards Petersburg, on the Appomatox River, which held large quantities of tobacco and military stores. Approaching Blandford, to the south-east, the British met about 1,000 militia, well entrenched, under Brigadier-General John Peter Muhlenberg. Feinting a frontal attack, Phillips sent Simcoe around Muhlenberg's right; American fire held off the British initially, until four guns were brought to bear on their right (at which point the flanking movement was detected). Muhlenberg then withdrew across the river, destroying the bridge after him. Losses were about 60 to 70 on each side. Phillips destroyed 4,000 hogsheads of tobacco and some small ships, but spared the buildings. (Courtesy: Colonial Williamsburg)

Action at Osborne's, 27 April 1781. Learning of an American flotilla and stores at Osborne's, Arnold left Petersburg with the 76th and 80th Foot, Queen's Rangers and Jäegers. Although surprised, the American commander refused to surrender. The British artillery (two 6-pdrs and two 3-pdrs) forced the supporting militia from the opposite bank, and together with the Jaegers' rifles, quickly silenced the *Tempest* (20 guns). The crews of the *Renown* (26) and *Jefferson* (14) then panicked and abandoned ship. Twelve vessels and considerable amounts of flour and naval stores were captured, another nine vessels and 2,000 hogsheads of tobacco were burned. The British suffered no casualties. (Courtesy: Colonial Williamsburg)

THE ALLIES MARCH SOUTH

The routes taken by the separate American and French Continentals on their way south.

naissance in force of the British lines. The raid warned Clinton of possible danger and prompted more letters to Cornwallis.

In mid-June, it had been suggested that a fleet under de Grasse would arrive in the North by late July; however, on 14 August, Rochambeau advised Washington that de Grasse would only come as far up as Chesapeake Bay, as he had to return to the Caribbean for the winter. At this, all plans to attack New York were abandoned in favour of a new plan: to move a combined force of 7,000 men to the head of the Elk River, then down Chesapeake Bay to Virginia to trap Cornwallis. It would involve leaving General Heath to hold the Hudson Highlands with New England militia and 4,000 Continentals (17 New England infantry regiments, some dragoons and one regiment of artillery), while the Allies marched south - ostensibly to mount an amphibious attack against either Staten Island or Sandy Hook.

On 19 August, 4,500 French and 2,000 Continentals marched north to King's Ferry. Crossing the Hudson River, they headed south in three columns, the Americans in the east and centre, the French to the west. Muddy roads delayed the French rearguard until 26 August, but as the whole forced concentrated at Chatham on 28 August, Washington calculated that the deceit could probably be maintained for one more day (even senior staff officers were still unaware of the true destination at this time), by which time the Americans had moved through Brunswick and Boundbrook and the French through Morristown.

On 30 August, the ruse was exposed as the columns veered off towards Princeton, which the Americans reached that evening. The next day, Hazen's Regiment and the 2nd New York arrived at Trenton, from where they guarded the passage of the artillery and engineers' equipages by boat to Wilmington, Delaware. The rest of the Allied force now combined into one column, and, with its precious head start on the enemy, began crossing the Delaware River on 1 September, with the Americans in the lead, and the French a day's march behind to keep down the clouds of dust that covered the men like snow.

On 2 September, the Americans by-passed Philadelphia, leaving the triumphal passage through the city to their French colleagues, who were fêted by politicians and public alike over the next two days. By 5 September, the American vanguard was reunited with Hazen's command; that same day, Washington learned that de Grasse had entered Chesapeake Bay and was waiting for him. Three days later, the entire army was at the head of the Elk River.

Meanwhile, Lafayette had been joined by St Simon's division, which de Grasse had transported from the West Indies. The combined force had ensured that Cornwallis neither escaped, nor discovered the Allies' objective. Wayne and his Pennsylvanians (on their way to join Greene) were recalled to Westover, and the North Carolina militia had been instructed to destroy every boat and ferry, and guard every crossing into Virginia. The arrival of Lauzun's cavalry (minus their commander) on 12 September meant that Lafayette and St Simon could not only match Cornwallis in numbers, but could also negate his previous superiority in mounted troops.

However, none of the protagonists were, as yet, aware of the drama that was unfolding beyond the entrance to Chesapeake Bay out into the Atlantic Ocean.

NAVAL OPERATIONS
MARCH TO OCTOBER 1781

As the king's soldiers marched and dug in the heat of the Virginian summer, his sailors also faced problems. The Royal Navy was expected to protect the king's subjects and their property; prevent the Americans importing military stores (and exporting goods to pay for them); transport troops to and around North America and keep them supplied; and combat the efforts of American privateers and the fleets of two major empires. In theory, around 200 warships were available for these tasks; in practice, government parsimony since 1763 had led to poorly maintained ships, insufficient repair facilities and materials, and shortages of manpower. And because the Admiralty under Lord Sandwich had immediately identified French (and Spanish) interest in using the rebellion to restore prestige at British expense, the Channel and Caribbean commands invariably took precedence over the American squadron – not least in the quality of its commanders.

Fortunately, Washington was having no better luck in obtaining naval co-operation. Without the necessary dockyard facilities to build and service line-of-battle ships, the Americans had to rely throughout the war on allies who were usually pursuing their own agenda – the inactivity of the seven ships that arrived with Rochambeau, under Chevalier de Ternay, was only partly due to the British blockade.

Following its virtual annihilation in the Seven Years' War, the French Navy had not only been rebuilt, but also redirected. Unlike the British, who needed strong reasons not to fight, French admirals saw their role as strategic, with the overall objective more important than risking all in the uncertainty of battle. This role even influenced them in battle, when their principal gunnery tactic was to dismast enemy vessels in order to prevent pursuit (whereas the British aimed at the hull to knock out guns and men, and then captured the vessel).

When de Ternay died in December 1780, his successor, Chevalier Destouches, proved equally conservative and cautious. When Arnold raided Virginia, Washington saw a chance to trap him between Lafayette's army and a French naval force in Chesapeake Bay; but a storm forced Arbuthnot's blockading squadron away on 19 February, and Destouches sent only one ship and two frigates. On reaching the Chesapeake, Arnold merely withdrew up the Elizabeth River and the French returned to Newport, achieving nothing beyond capturing HMS *Romulus* (44 guns).

CAPES BATTLE (I)

The action off the Capes between Arbuthnot and Destouches on 16 March.

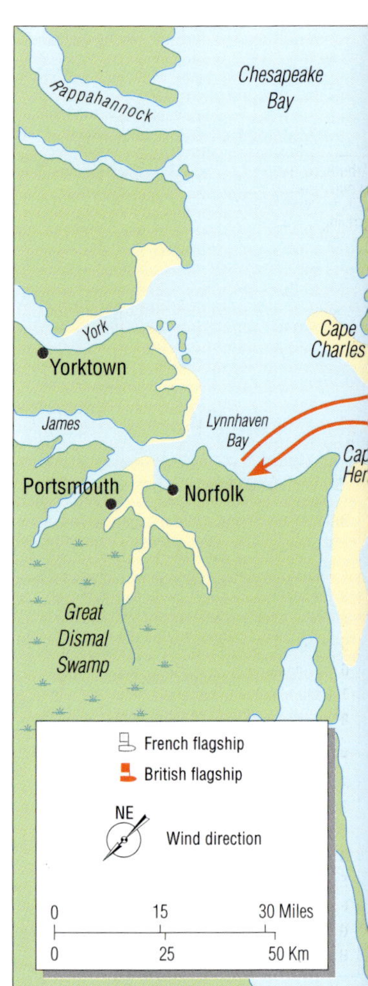

THE FIRST ACTION OFF THE CAPES

Frustrated by French inaction, Washington went to Newport and was delighted to observe Destouches' entire squadron, with 1,200 troops aboard, sail for Chesapeake Bay on 8 March in a further attempt to trap Arnold. Arbuthnot, anchored at the east end of Long Island, was informed and set off in pursuit 36 hours later, but when the fleets sighted each other off the Capes at dawn on 16 March, the British were leading (probably because the French ships were not 'coppered'[6]). Heavy seas, drizzle and a westerly wind prevented either side entering Chesapeake Bay, so at 7:00 am Arbuthnot signalled his ships to set more sail and form line of battle. As the British turned about, the French formed line and headed into the Atlantic; by 1:00pm, when the weather had worsened and the wind shifted to the north-east, both sides were in line ahead heading east-south-east.

Although each line contained eight major vessels, the British were slightly superior, having the only 90-gun ship, while the French had to include a heavy frigate (the recently-taken *Romulus*) to equalise the lines. About 2:00pm, the leading British ship, HMS *Robust*, was about to overhaul the rearmost enemy ship, *Eveille*, when the French executed a 180-degree turn around the British line, giving them the advantage of the weather gauge (this meant they could use their lower-deck guns, while those of the British – to windward – were dangerously close to the waterline as the ships heeled over).

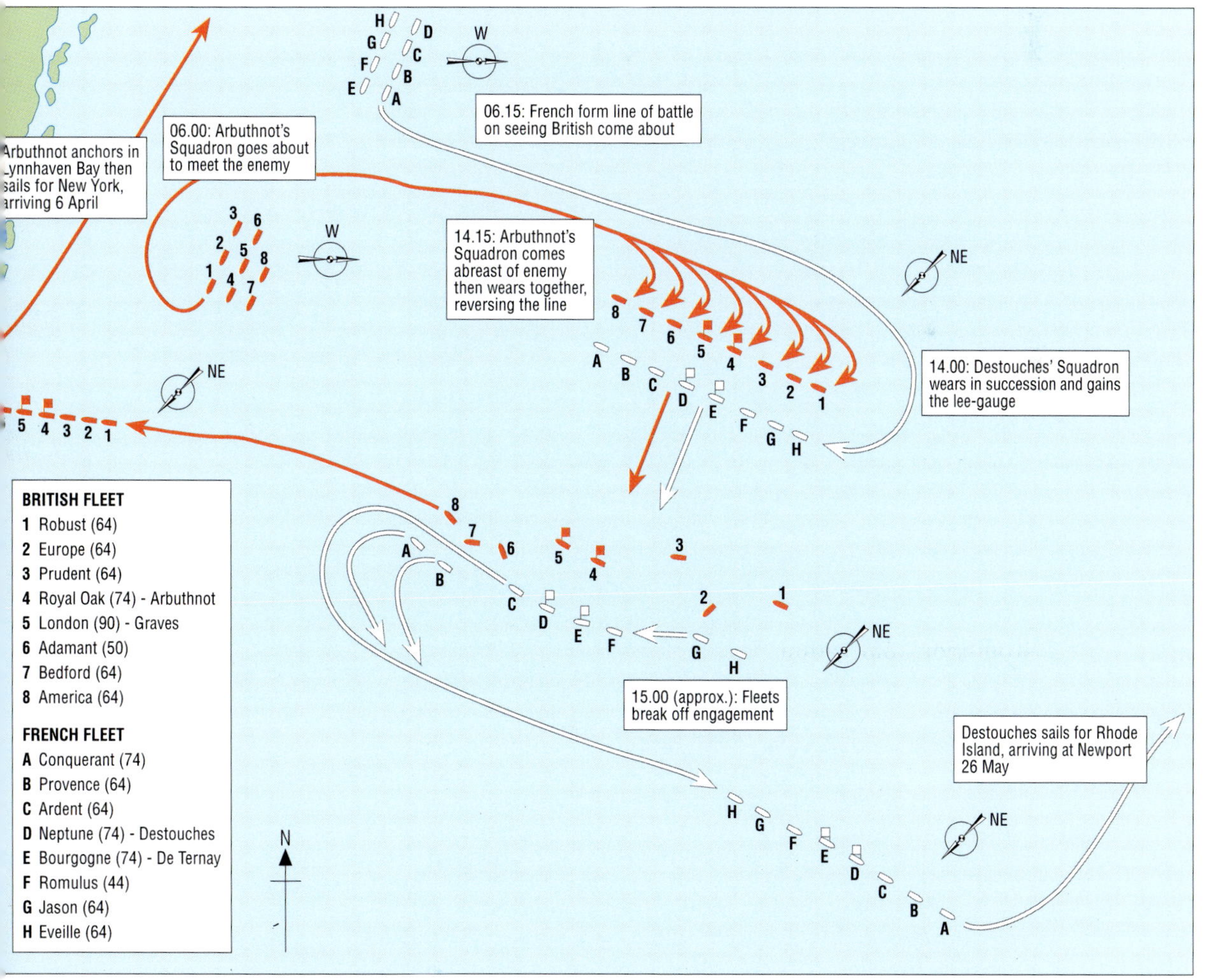

Almost immediately, *Robust* turned onto the same course and within 15 minutes had engaged the leading French ship, *Conquérant*, but also forced the other British ships to wear together (reversing their line). In the ensuing confusion, the French severely damaged the *Robust, Europe* and *Prudent*; their own van, particularly *Conquérant* and *Provence*, also suffered, and Destouches ordered both vessels to steer east-south-east, and signalled the rest of the line to tack in succession, while concentrating their fire on the three damaged ships of the British van. Arbuthnot wanted to chase after them, but his three leading ships were so badly damaged that he had no choice but to continue westwards into Chesapeake Bay, while the French returned to Rhode Island, arriving on 26 March.

The British lost 30 dead and 73 wounded, the French 72 dead and 112 wounded. Destouches, with superior control over his ships had outmanoeuvred and outfought Arbuthnot, then thrown away his advantage by returning to Newport – handing Arbuthnot a strategic victory he did not deserve and probably saving Arnold's neck (literally). Arbuthnot had failed to utilise his ships' superior speed and gunnery in the morning by not allowing his captains to engage the enemy at will; in the afternoon, he had neither ordered 'close action', nor removed the signal to 'maintain line of battle', thus preventing a general chase.

The British fleet returned to New York on 6 April, in the vain hope of repairing their ships. Arbuthnot spent most of April and May blockading Newport, deliberately avoiding Clinton, who wanted to attack the base before its fortifications became too strong. In June, Clinton wrote to Rodney expressing his fears – particularly in relation to a combined attack on New York – after captured letters indicated that Rear-Admiral de Grasse would sail to the Caribbean in spring, and then to America that summer (during the Caribbean hurricane season).

On 4 July, Rear-Admiral Thomas Graves took over from Arbuthnot, who returned to Great Britain in ill-health. Graves supported Clinton's plan for a base in the Chesapeake: he thought it would provide more suitable winter quarters for his squadron and it would be easier to obtain provisions there. On 21 July, the squadron sailed from Sandy Hook to intercept a French supply fleet heading for Boston, but missed it; when Graves returned, almost a month later, he found a letter from Rodney informing him that a French force was heading north and Hood was heading for the Chesapeake. While the danger to Cornwallis was acknowledged, nobody in New York or London appeared to consider the strategic consequences of his being overwhelmed. Yet throughout August, Clinton and Graves discussed a plan to attack Newport as if de Grasse's impending arrival was of little or no consequence[7].

THE STAGE IS SET

De Grasse had left Brest at the end of March with 21 ships of the line and a large convoy. Evading a squadron of 18 ships under Rear-Admiral Samuel Hood, he raised the blockade of Martinique, then sailed after Hood, but failed to catch him (again, many French ships were not coppered). As Hood rejoined Rodney at Antigua, de Grasse captured Tobago on 2 June; the two fleets then circled each other for several weeks before de Grasse anchored at Haiti on 26 July, where he received word from Washington and Rochambeau.

On 7 July Rodney wrote to Graves warning that a French force – probably a dozen ships – would be heading north and suggesting he rendezvous off the Capes with the squadron he was sending under Hood. Unfortunately the despatch was intercepted and Graves did not learn its contents until mid-August, by when illness had forced Rodney to return to England (with three ships), leaving Hood in command of the Caribbean squadron. This was a crippling blow: at that time Rodney was probably the most capable commander on either side in that part of the world. Hood was also talented, but he was junior to Graves (in a service where seniority was all); and of the 21 ships that Rodney had theoretically left behind, only 14 were available and fit for service.

Rear Admiral Samuel Hood (1724-1816), by J Northcote. Hood entered the Royal Navy in 1741, serving as a midshipman under Rodney, with whom he served again in 1759, thwarting a French invasion of England. In 1778, he was plucked from the obscurity of commissioner of Portsmouth Dockyard and governor of the Naval Academy, and sent to the West Indies as second-in-command of the Caribbean squadron. He proved himself an effective and able leader, though his fit of pique with Graves and childish refusal to give advice after the initial engagement with de Grasse may have helped to lose eight vital days. After the war, Hood became an admiral; on the outbreak of the French Revolution, he was given command of the Royalist forces in Toulon, which he was forced to abandon by superior Republican artillery under Major Bonaparte. (Courtesy: National Maritime Museum, Greenwich)

On 5 August, de Grasse left Haiti with 26 ships and five frigates, carrying 3,200 troops under Maj. Gen. Marquis de St Simon. Adopting an indirect course to confuse the British and rendezvous with reinforcements, he sailed north between Florida and the Bahamas, capturing three British ships (*Corp Morrant* (24), *Queen Charlotte* (18), and *Sandwich* (34)) to prevent his whereabouts being detected.

Hood had sailed with 14 ships and several other vessels five days after de Grasse. Taking a more direct route and enjoying better weather, he arrived in Chesapeake Bay on 21 August, five days before his opponent. Finding neither the enemy, nor reinforcements from Graves, Hood sailed for New York, aware that the British had to concentrate their forces to have any chance of giving battle. On the day that he arrived (28 August), news also came in that the French squadron at Newport – commanded by Admiral Comte de Barras, who had recently returned from France – had put to sea on 25 August. This made the plan to attack Newport redundant and although Graves assumed, correctly, that the two French fleets planned to meet at the Chesapeake, his five ships did not cross the bar at Sandy Hook to join Hood until 31 August. They then headed south, hoping to catch de Barras and his fleet of eight ships, four frigates and 18 transports (carrying Rochambeau's siege train), but arrived off the Chesapeake well ahead of the Frenchman, who had initially sailed well out into the Atlantic in order to avoid interception.

Meanwhile, de Grasse had arrived in Chesapeake Bay on 30 August and anchored his fleet in three lines in Lynnhaven Bay. After sending four ships to blockade Yorktown, he began ferrying St Simon's corps up the James River to reinforce Lafayette, and sent smaller ships up the Chesapeake to meet the troops from New York.

THE SECOND ACTION OFF THE CAPES

Around mid-morning on 5 September, the frigate *Aigrette* signalled de Grasse's flagship *Ville de Paris* that ten sail (later corrected to 20) were approaching from the north-east. Initial elation at the assumption that it was de Barras soon dissolved, to be replaced by frantic signals to the 1,900 men ashore looking for forage and firewood when it became obvious that the force could only be British. At 11:00am Graves signalled his squadron to form line of battle (with each ship at a distance of two cable lengths) and headed for the entrance to the Chesapeake.

De Grasse determined to put to sea and fight, knowing that if he allowed the British into the Chesapeake, Cornwallis might be rescued and the Allied army might itself then be at risk; equally, the British would probably capture the fleet of de Barras, who was expected at any moment. At 11:30am de Grasse ordered his fleet to prepare to put to sea with the aim of drawing the British away from the Chesapeake, even though the shore parties would not return in time. Each ship still had around 80 men and all its boats missing[8]; on the *Citoyen*, for example, the upper-deck guns were left unmanned as over 200 officers and men were absent. The French had to wait until noon for the tide to turn, and

CAPES BATTLE (II)

The action off the Capes between Graves and de Grasse on 5-13 September

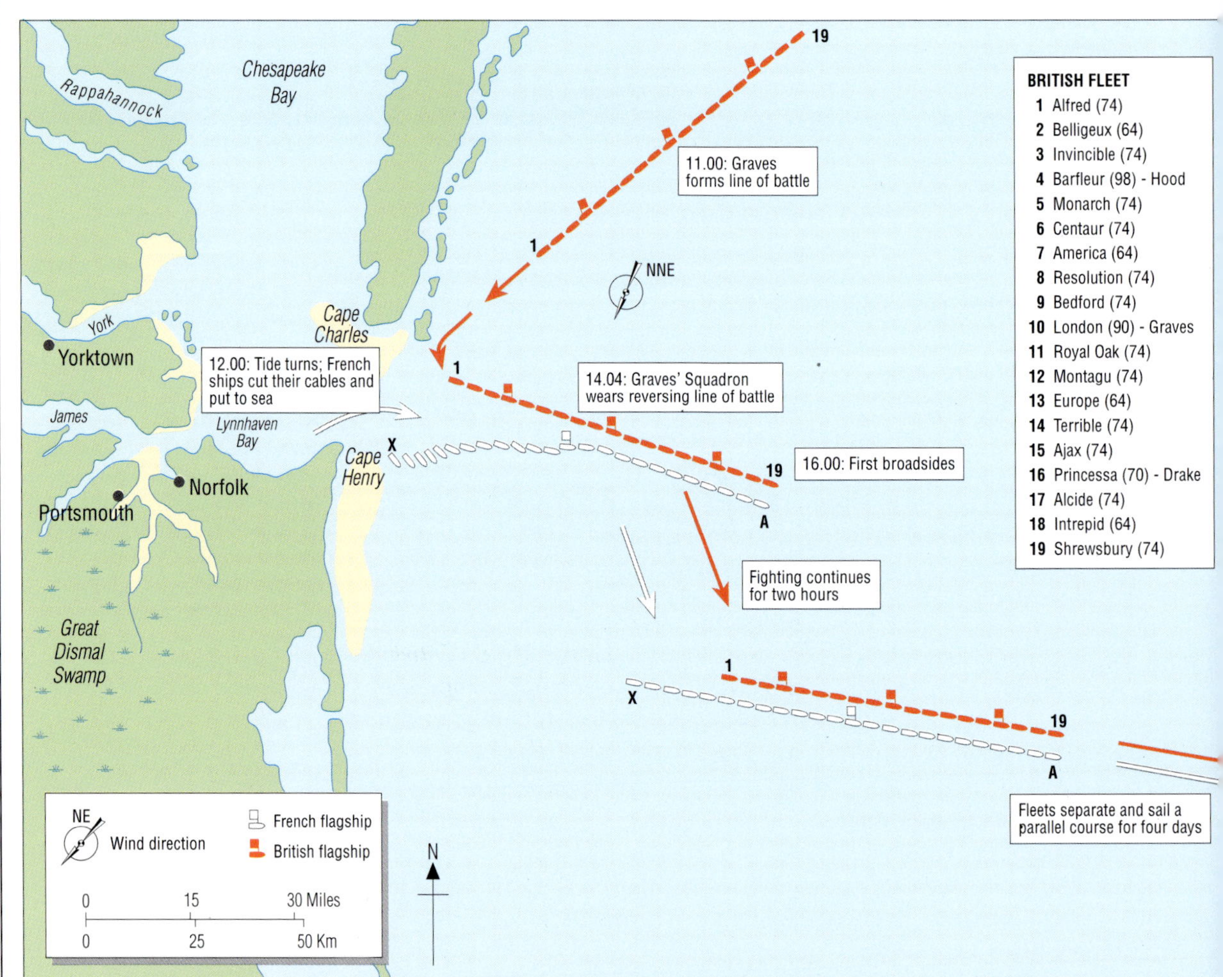

because of their dispositions in Lynnhaven Bay, they were forced to reverse their normal battle line. Eventually, they emerged in some sort of order, having carefully negotiated the shoals in the channel between Cape Charles and Cape Henry.

The two fleets were less evenly matched than the numbers suggested (24 French ships against 19 British), even allowing for the missing French crews – though the British were also short-handed. The French had the lee gauge and so could use all their gun decks, while the British, to windward, had to keep their lower ports closed. Although the French ships were slower, due to not being copper-bottomed, they had heavier guns, and, most crucially as it transpired, the French ships were in a better state of repair. One British ship, HMS *Terrible*, was already having trouble staying afloat and others were also suffering from the shortage of naval stores in New York.

At 2:00pm Graves saw the French emerging from Chesapeake Bay in a straggling line-ahead formation, with the van slightly separated from the centre and rear. Rather than fall upon the French and force the type of 'pell-mell' battle in which British gunnery usually triumphed, Graves decided to follow the Admiralty's 'Fighting Instructions' and, seeing his fleet approaching a large shoal at the entrance to the bay (called the Middle Ground) made the preparative signal to wear. At 2:15pm, he ordered his ships from a south-westerly course onto one roughly parallel to the French; this would let de Grasse's centre come abreast of his own and allow each British ship to engage the vessel opposite to it. However, it also reversed the British line, placing Graves' best commander, Hood, furthest from the enemy and his weakest ships opposite the enemy's strong van, as well as giving de Grasse more time to reorganise.

As the two fleets drew closer, Graves ordered the rearmost ships to make more sail and close up, and around 3:45pm, with the two vans closing, he signalled 'close action', ordering his fleet to bear down and engage their opposite numbers. At 4:05pm, with the fleets about ten miles off the Capes, the second British ship, HMS *Intrepid*, opened fire on the second French ship, *Marseilles*, and within ten minutes the entire van and part of the centre were engaging the French.

Although the French van was initially outnumbered, the British had the worst of it, with the leading ship, HMS *Shrewsbury*, hammered by the *Pluton*, losing 14 dead and 36 injured, including the captain and first lieutenant. As HMS

Intrepid tried to cover, it received 65 holes on the starboard side, losing 25 dead and 35 wounded. The weakest British ship, HMS *Terrible*, was also shot up and was taking on a foot of water every 10 minutes, while the *Auguste* approached close enough to Drake's flagship, HMS *Princessa*, to have boarded it.

The action lasted about two hours, and with the two fleets on converging, rather than parallel, courses, virtually all of the fighting fell on the vans and centres. In fact, Hood's rear division hardly fired a shot, largely due to the confusion caused by Graves's signals (and not helped by the ships of the American and Caribbean squadrons using different signals!). Initially, Graves signalled 'line of battle', with each ship a single cable length apart to stop the numerically superior French from slipping through and overwhelming individual vessels from two sides. However, he then added 'close action', which flew simultaneously until (according to Hood and others) about 5:25pm.

The dual signal caused no problems for the van and – as time progressed – the centre, since, being in close contact with the enemy, the two commands were perfectly compatible. But it was impossible for Hood's division to do both, as his angle of approach would require him to break the line in order to close. Since the 'Fighting Instructions' accorded precedence to maintaining the line of battle, he preserved the line and so arrived too late. Graves insisted that the 'line of battle' signal was directed at those vessels bunching around his flagship, HMS *London* (which was probably true), but there is no doubt that it caused confusion, as Hood was not a man to shirk a fight.

The British had 90 killed, 246 wounded and 16 guns (just over 1 per cent of their total) dismounted; French losses were a little over 200. French gunnery tactics had all but disabled five of the leading British

ABOVE AND RIGHT

The Battle off The Capes, 5-13 September 1781. Despite the tendency of all paintings of naval battles to look the same, the right hand view (whether by accident or design) shows the vans of the fleets on a converging course as a result of their respective manoeuvres earlier that morning. Prior to the introduction of 'the Nelson touch', the standard tactic was to fight broadside-to-broadside in

parallel lines, invariably ensuring, as on this occasion, that neither side gained a clear advantage. The decision by de Grasse to emerge and give battle proved correct. By forcing the British away from the mouth of the Capes, he allowed de Barras (with the French siege train) to enter Lynnhaven Bay unmolested, and drew Graves away from Cornwallis.
(Courtesy: Mariners' Museum, Newport and US Navy, Hampton)

ships – HMS *Shrewsbury, Intrepid, Ajax, Alcide* and *Terrible* – and though the leading French vessels were also damaged, de Grasse kept his numerical superiority. More importantly, with both fleets now heading away from the Capes, he also still held the strategic advantage.

With the crews of the leading ships on both sides exhausted, firing died down around dusk, though the fleets maintained contact through the night. On the morning of 6 September, British observers felt that the French fleet looked the less badly damaged. Graves did not know what to do next: resume the battle, return to New York, or head for the Chesapeake? Hood, by far the superior tactician and strategist, was angered by Graves's tactics the previous day, but now made the situation worse by refusing to give advice out of a fit of pique.

For the next two days, the fleets remained in sight of each other, with Graves increasingly aware that he was in the wrong place, but many of his ships were still unable to manoeuvre properly. On the evening of 9 September de Grasse turned north-west, back to Chesapeake Bay, having achieved his two aims of drawing Graves away and allowing de Barras to enter the Chesapeake. On the morning of 11 September he entered the Chesapeake to find de Barras at anchor in Lynnhaven Bay.

Meanwhile, the British fleet had continued on into the Atlantic, having been forced to burn HMS *Terrible*, which was too badly damaged to be saved. On 12 September, Graves sent the frigate HMS *Medea* to look into Chesapeake Bay; the next day, her captain reported a much larger French force than Graves had engaged a week earlier. At this point, all three British admirals agreed to sail to New York for repairs and the badly damaged squadron arrived off Sandy Hook on 20 September.

When Cornwallis's predicament had become apparent at the start of September, Clinton believed that he could hold out until the end of

October; in two letters from Yorktown, dated 16 and 17 September, Cornwallis himself suggested six weeks, but his estimate of 36 enemy ships in Chesapeake Bay put serious doubts in Clinton's mind that there were enough British ships in North America to oppose them. Nevertheless, on 24 September, a council of war of the senior army and naval officers in New York, recommended that once Graves's ships were repaired – probably by 5 October – 5,000 troops be embarked and sent to relieve Cornwallis.

Despite a reinforcement of three ships under Rear-Admiral Robert Digby, the idea of an amphibious operation to rescue Cornwallis was still being uneasily debated by the Royal Navy, despite apparent unanimity at the councils of war. Digby, who had arrived from England to take command from Graves (who was to go to Jamaica), courteously subordinated himself to Graves until the present campaign was over, but as the repairs proceeded painfully slowly, relations between them became as bad as those between Graves and Hood.

Although the rescue operation was agreed to be the highest priority, at another council of war on September 30, Graves indicated that repairs would not be completed until 12 October. His correspondence with Clinton increasingly suggested that he was not keen on the *modus operandi* proposed by the council (an attitude that led to fierce arguments between Graves and Hood and Digby). Privately, Clinton began to believe that he might have to relieve Cornwallis by attacking Philadelphia without the help of the Royal Navy.

In fact, the lack of a proper dockyard at New York, a succession of accidents, and shortages of naval stores and provisions delayed the departure of the expedition until 19 October, when 28 ships (including three of 50 guns) and eight frigates sailed from Sandy Hook with 7,149 troops embarked in transports. Even as they sailed, it was still unclear if they would arrive in time to save Cornwallis, or if Graves could force his way past de Grasse and into Chesapeake Bay at all.

This modern painting shows Arnold conferring with his officers during the raid on Richmond in January 1781. The other mounted figure is possibly an orderly, about to ride off with the message to Jefferson offering to spare Richmond if British ships were allowed to sail up the James River and carry away tobacco and other stores (much of which had been confiscated from Loyalists). (Courtesy: Colonial Williamsburg)

THE NOOSE TIGHTENS

On 14 September Washington and Rochambeau arrived at Williamsburg, having spent three days at Mount Vernon (Washington's first visit home in six years). Their men were now moving down from the head of the Elk River and de Grasse despatched frigates to collect Lincoln's division and the French. By 26 September, the whole force was at Williamsburg; the following day, Washington issued his orders for the advance on Yorktown.

Early on 28 September, the Allies set off. Muhlenberg's light infantry, Moylan's dragoons and Lewis's riflemen formed the American advance guard; a group of volunteers and a battalion of converged flank companies preceded the French column. The force, ready for action in 'light marching order', divided at Halfway House, the Americans moving right to join Nelson's militia, the French going left. The line advanced to within two miles of Yorktown, then halted before the first line of defences.

The British Light Infantry on the Allies' left were forced back by de Laval's chasseurs, supported by two field guns and Baron de Viomenil's division. Tarleton's Legion, covering the British left behind a stream, came under ineffective long-range artillery fire and retired to the Moore House. That night, the Allied army 'lay on its arms'.

On 29 September, the Allies manoeuvred into a crescent-shaped line, the contingents separated by Beaverdam (Warwick) Creek, which the engineers had bridged during the night. As American skirmishers recon-

ABOVE AND LEFT **American infantry and cavalry, by Baron von Closen, an aide-de-camp to Rocham-beau. His eyewitness drawings, though crude, are useful contemporary records of American uniforms, and show (from right to left): a gunner of a Continental artillery regiment, a rifleman, a centre company man from Hazen's Canadian Regiment, and a black private from a Rhode Island light infantry company, together with the light dragoon (above), are representative of the units which formed the American advance guard (under Muhlenberg, Moylan and Lewis) on the march from Williamsburg to Yorktown. (Courtesy: Anne S K Brown Military Collection, Providence)**

A view of the British lines from the south. The British positions were enlarged substantially by the Confederates in 1862, and so, other than their approximate positions, the present-day remains are not intended to be an accurate reconstruction (unlike the Allied siege lines). The Hornwork is on the left, covering the Hampton Road into Yorktown, and showing its commanding aspect. The southern sector of the line stretches away to the right (roughly where Redoubts No.6-8 would have been sited). Redoubt No.9 is just to the left of the small tree at the far right. In 1781, the view was much clearer, as the trees had been cut down and the fresh earthworks were easier to see. (Author's photograph)

noitred the British positions, especially those held by the Anspachers on the British left, the Allies formed up in their allocated areas as their commanders examined the terrain and pronounced it very favourable for a siege.

Since his arrival at Yorktown, Cornwallis had his men (and the numbers of slaves who had joined him) building a defensive line around Yorktown, with a covered way inside it to allow troops to move safely around the perimeter. The defences included ten redoubts: Nos. 1 and 2 lay outside the town overlooking the steep banks of Yorktown Creek and facing the river road to Williamsburg; Nos. 3, 4 and 5 faced inland, overlooking the ravine behind the town; beside them was the Hornwork, a more substantial defence designed to cover the Hampton Road into Yorktown; Nos. 6 to 8 faced south-east towards Wormley Creek; while Nos. 9 and 10 stood 200-300 yards outside the main line, commanding a small mound and the beach below the cliffs, respectively. Minor works were built in Yorktown, to cover the roads and gulleys, along with 14 batteries mounting 65 guns – including 18-pdrs. taken from ships in the harbour.

Over the river, Gloucester Point was also fortified, though less heavily with four redoubts, 20 guns in three batteries and a stockade by the beach. Beyond the lines, flèches (chevron-shaped works with an open rear) covered roads and gulleys.

Because of the time needed to complete these defences and the nature of the surrounding terrain, more works had been constructed, and trees felled, in the Pigeon Quarter, a mile-wide neck between Yorktown and Wormley Creeks. Here, a redoubt commanded the

The Fusilier Redoubt. The remains of the Fusilier (or Star) Redoubt, which guarded the River Road into the town from Williamsburg, as seen by the French. Over half the original work has been lost through natural erosion over the years. (Author's photograph)

Hampton road, with two others astride the Williamsburg road, along with batteries and flèches. Further entrenchments were constructed north-east of Yorktown, including a large star-shaped redoubt (later called the Fusilier Redoubt) to cover the river road, supported by the frigate HMS *Guadeloupe*; and also around Moore's Mill at the head of Wormley Creek.

THE SIEGE BEGINS

The following day – 30 September – the Allies awoke to find the outer defences abandoned and the enemy inside Yorktown. Although widely criticised for this move, Cornwallis was outnumbered three to one, weakened by sickness and the detachments at Gloucester, and liable to be outflanked if the Allies crossed Wormley Creek. Allied numbers, and a letter from Clinton promising relief by 5 October, also suggested that consolidating within Yorktown was a sound move.

The Allies seized the works, French chasseurs occupying the Pigeon Quarter, while Lafayette's division took the Hampton Road redoubt and converted an adjacent battery into a fourth redoubt during the night. St Simon's volunteers drove British pickets away from the Fusilier Redoubt, losing one dead and three wounded. The only American casualty was Lt. Col. Scammel, who was mortally wounded while investigating the abandoned redoubts; taken into Yorktown for attention, he was returned to his own lines, but died on 6 October.

Under heavy fire – some 350 rounds on 2 October alone – the conversion was completed in four days with little loss (although one roundshot killed four Pennsylvanians). The Allies then began their own works: within a week, some 6,000 stakes, 2,000 fascines and 600 gabions were manufactured, while the Allied siege trains were brought up from Williamsburg with the help of officers' horses. In order to avoid confusion during work on the main siege line, von Steuben devised precise orders for the fatigue and covering parties, including posting sentries to warn of enemy shells, so that the men could take cover. Morale was high and desertion by American troops ceased entirely when Washington promised summary execution to anyone captured in Yorktown.

At Gloucester, Weedon's militia brigade was reinforced by Lauzun's corps on 28 September, and 800 marines under de Choisy from the French fleet. The passive Weedon was undiplomatically displaced by the more aggressive Frenchmen, who advanced on the town. On 3 October Tarleton led a foraging expedition by the Legion cavalry, Queen's Rangers Infantry and 17th Foot light company. Returning along Severn Road (which was four miles long and enclosed by fields), he saw de Choisy's main group entering the lane as he reached the south end a mile from Gloucester, and decided on a rearguard action to allow the wagons to reach the town.

Placing the infantry in a wood on his right, he charged Lauzun's hussars with his Legion troop as they emerged from the lane. In the ensuing skirmish Tarleton was dismounted, but as Lauzun rode up to capture him, the other three British troops arrived and Tarleton escaped. Lauzun pursued, but was forced to retire by the British infantry; Tarleton followed up, only to be checked by Lauzun's infantry, then

THE ALLIES ADVANCE ON YORKTOWN AND GLOUCESTER 28 SEPTEMBER - 3 OCTOBER, 1781

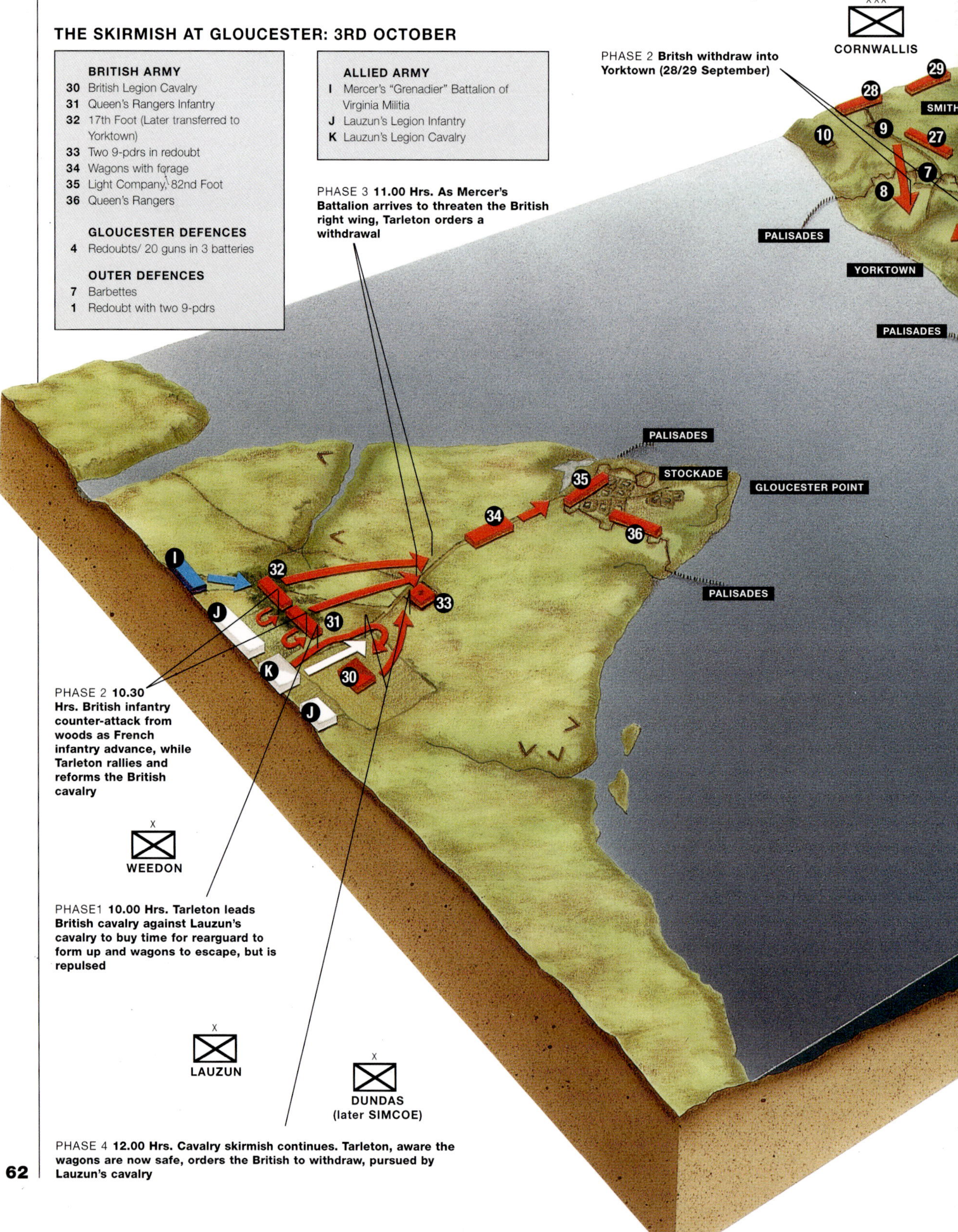

THE ALLIES ADVANCE ON YORKTOWN: 28-30 SEPTEMBER

BRITISH ARMY

13 33rd Foot
14 23rd Foot
15 43rd Foot
16 Foot Guards
17 80th Foot
18 76th Foot
19 Four 6-pdrs
20 Four 3-pdrs
21 2nd Light Infantry
22 1st Light Infantry
23 British Legion Cavalry & Infantry (Transferred to Gloucester 1 October)
24 1st Anspach-Bayreuth Regiment
25 2nd Anspach-Bayreuth Regiment
26 Anspach-Bayreuth Artillery
27 Regt. von Bose
28 Regt. Prince Hereditaire
29 71st Foot

OUTER DEFENCES (PIGEON QUATER)

(i) Redoubt
(ii) Redoubt - Two 12-pdrs
(iii) Redoubt - Two 12-pdrs
(iv) Barbette - Two 9-pdrs

INNER DEFENCES (YORKTOWN)

1-10 Redoubts
11 Star (or Fusilier) Redoubt
12 Hornwork (Hampton Road)

ALLIED ARMY

A Moylan's Dragoons
B Muhlenberg's Light Infantry Brigade
C Lewis's Rifle Companies
D Belzunce Dragoons
E Volontaires de St Simon
F Laval's Flank Battalion (grenadier/chasseur companies)
G Regiment Saintonge
H Regiment Soisonnais

brought up his own foot. A long-range musketry duel ensued, until a flanking party (a hussar company and a veteran militia battalion under the experienced Lt. Col. Mercer) arrived on the British right via a hidden track that joined Severn Road at its south end, whereupon Tarleton withdrew.

The Allies camped on the battlefield, sending out strong pickets. Casualties were surprisingly light: 12 British dead or captured; three French dead and 16 wounded. Though the convoy arrived safely, it was the last – the British could now only be supplied by sea.

RIGHT **Lieutenant-Colonel Alexander Hamilton (1757-1804) by A Chappel. Originally an artillery officer, at 20 Hamilton became Washington's secretary and aide-de-camp, but argued with him in 1781, and took a field command during the Yorktown campaign, leading one of the battalions formed from Scammell's regiment. As officer of the day, on 14 October, he forced Lafayette to give him command of the attack on Redoubt 10. (Courtesy: Museum of the City of New York)**

THE LAST ACT

On 6 October the Allies began digging the first parallel, which would run 2,000 yards from the Pigeon Quarter to the river, some 600-800 yards from the main British line (the greater distance being in front of redoubts Nos. 9 and 10). The ravine west of the town dictated that the approach be made from the south-east, limiting the frontage and amount of digging involved.

At dusk, 4,300 Allied troops marched to the designated areas, led by Lincoln and Baron de Viomenil, with the French to the left of the Hampton Road. As 1,500 men dug, the rest lay under arms to repel any sorties and by first light the works were deep enough to protect those digging during daylight. Casualties were 20 killed and wounded, all but four on the French left, where a deserter alerted the British to a feint by

BELOW **The First Parallel from behind the Allied Lines. The main trench line, looking west towards the French Grand Battery. The area to the right is the approximate position of the bizarre parade undertaken by Hamilton's light infantry battalion. To the right of the tree, the Hornwork can just be made out in the far distance. (Author's photograph)**

Brigadier-General Henry Knox (1750-1806), by C W Peale. After hastening the British departure from Boston with his famous 'noble train of artillery', Knox continued to render valuable service to Washington and, by 1781, had created a highly professional artillery corps. A far more able administrator than he was a battlefield tactician, his over-reaction to the promotion of rivals never outweighed his loyalty to the cause. (Courtesy: Independence National Historical Park, Philadelphia)

the Touraine Regiment against the Fusilier Redoubt, to cover the construction of works by the river.

On 7 October Lafayette's division had the honour of entering the trenches first, with colours flying and drums beating – and a bizarre display of arms drill by Hamilton's battalion on the exposed parapet. By 9 October, four redoubts and five batteries had been added, with surprisingly few casualties (although fever was widespread, especially among the French). The Allies could not understand Cornwallis's passivity; in fact he was unprepared for such a siege and his own sick list already exceeded 1,000 men.

As work progressed, von Steuben issued more detailed orders for covering parties, down to how each platoon should respond to an attack. Knox also arranged for an artillery field officer to be in the trenches to aim each gun, and record the rounds fired and their effect.

At 3:00pm on 9 October, the French opened fire on the Fusilier Redoubt with four 12-pdrs. and six mortars and howitzers, forcing HMS *Guadeloupe* away to Gloucester. The first American guns (six 18- and 24-pdrs., four mortars, two howitzers) began firing from the battery by the river two hours later, Washington supposedly firing the first shot. An early target was the house used by Cornwallis as his headquarters, which was soon in ruins.

The following day, the 'Grand French Battery' on the left of the parallel (ten 18- and 24-pdrs., six mortars) and the second American battery (four 18-pdrs., two mortars) opened fire. Lafayette – again officer of the day (he, Lincoln and von Steuben taking turns) – asked Governor Nelson for a suitable target. He immediately suggested his home as the

ABOVE **A French battery in action. Despite the distinctly 'Napoleonic' look of the uniforms, this gives a good idea of activity in a battery (though esprit de corps would probably prevent quite as much debris being left lying around). (Courtesy: Anne S K Brown Military Collection, Providence)**

most likely to house Cornwallis. HMS *Charon* and two transports were set alight and sunk by the guns of the Touraine work on the night of 10 October. By morning, 52 Allied guns were firing and Cornwallis wrote to Clinton that casualties had reached 70.

On the night of 11 October, von Steuben's and Baron de Viomenil's divisions began the second parallel just 350 yards from Yorktown. Despite false alarms and accidents from Allied guns firing over their heads, by dawn they had completed a trench 750 yards long, seven feet

LAFAYETTE'S MEN ENTER THE TRENCHES, 7 OCTOBER 1781
Having forced Cornwallis back into Yorktown, the Allies sited the first parallel some 600 yards from the British defences. On the following morning, the trenches were occupied for the first time; in the American sector, the honour went to Lafayette's light infantry division, which marched in colours flying and drums beating. As the battalions took their places, Lt. Col. Alexander Hamilton ordered his New York and Connecticut companies to " . . . mount the bank, front the enemy, and there by word of command go through all the ceremony of soldiery, ordering and grounding our arms." Although Hamilton's officers were unimpressed by his wanton exposure of his men, it clearly had some effect on the British, as " . . . although the enemy had been firing a little before, they did not now give us a single shot." (Adam Hook)

TOP AND CENTRE
The view today. These two views show the reconstructed French Grand Battery in the Allies' first parallel, which included some thirty guns, howitzers and mortars. The first is a gunner's view of the British line just to the right of the Hornwork, somewhere between Redoubts 6 and 7. The second shows the view of the French position from the 'receiving end', some 800 yards away inside the Hornwork (at right). The French battery can just be discerned at the base of the treeline in the dead centre of the photo – the white dot in the trees is the regimental flag of the Auxonne Regiment of artillery planted in the parapet. (Author's photographs)

BELOW **The Nelson House, the home of Governor Thomas Nelson, signatory of the Declaration of Independence, and commander of the Virginia militia during the siege, which still bears the marks of direct hits. This house should not be confused with that of Secretary Nelson, which was so badly damaged at the start of the bombardment that its occupant was allowed to return to the Allied Lines, where he gave the gunners valuable information (the ruins of this house lie just inside the Hornwork). (Author's photograph)**

wide and almost four feet deep. Two more days saw the task almost finished, except for the section by the river containing redoubts Nos. 9 and 10. Clearly these had to be incorporated, and the task of capturing them went to the élite of each army: Lafayette's Light Infantry and the flank companies of Baron de Viomenil's regiments. The assaults would take place on the night of 14 October.

The French attack on redoubt No. 9 (the larger work which held 120 British and Hessians) involved 400 men from the Deux Ponts and Gatenois regiments under Lt. Col. Count Guillaume de Deux Ponts, with the Gatenois second battalion under Col. Count de Rostaing in reserve. Upon the signal (six shells in quick succession, around 8:00 pm), they advanced in columns by platoons led by Deux Ponts with his second in command, Lt. Col. L'Estrade of Gatenois and two Deux Ponts chasseur sergeants, all four men having inspected the ground the previous night.

RIGHT **A view of the first parallel from in front of the Allied Lines. The photograph shows the Allied first parallel directly to the south of Yorktown, with (left to right) the two American batteries and the French Grand Battery. The lighter grass in the foreground marks the position of a sap used in the construction of the second parallel, and later as a 'covered way' to the second parallel after the capture of Redoubt No. 9 (some 200 yards behind the viewer) and No. 10. (Author's photograph)**

RIGHT **Washington and Rochambeau (left) issue orders to their respective commands, possibly for the attacks on the two redoubts on 14/15 October. Although somewhat over-dramatic, this print is exceptional in being fairly good on uniform details. (Courtesy: Anne S K Brown Collection, Providence)**

Some 50 Gatenois chasseurs quickly followed, with fascines and ladders.

Eighty yards from the work they were challenged by a German sentry; rushing on, they were stopped by the abbatis and lost time – and men –as the pioneers cut through it. The first officer on the parapet was shot in the legs; L'Estrade was knocked into the ditch by a wounded soldier and Deux Ponts also fell when the officer helping him was mortally wounded. As they mounted the parapet, the garrison counterattacked, but quickly surrendered. The action lasted under 30 minutes and French casualties were 15 dead and 77 wounded[9]; the garrison lost 18 dead and 50 captured, the rest escaping.

Barely 100 yards away, 400 men of Gimat's, Hamilton's and Laurens's Light Infantry battalions, with some sappers, approached redoubt No. 10, held by 70 British troops. At the signal the column advanced with unloaded muskets, led by Hamilton (who had gone to Washington over

STORMING OF REDOUBT NO. 9, 14/15 OCTOBER 1781

The honour of storming the stronger of the two outlying redoubts went to the French. As the sappers cleared the abbatis and palisade, the Gatenois chasseurs threw their fascines into the ditch and scrambled up the parapet. Despite heavy casualties among the officers, the French took the work after 30 minutes of fierce hand-to-hand fighting. (Adam Hook)

Lafayette's head on hearing that the Frenchman Gimat was to command) and a 'forlorn hope' of 20 men. The Light Infantry division and two Pennsylvania battalions formed the reserve.

With Laurens's two companies enveloping the rear of the work, the main group charged past and through the abbatis. Within 10 minutes, the redoubt was captured with a loss of nine dead and 31 wounded (six of the latter being officers); their retreat cut off, all the British were killed or captured.

No sooner were the works taken than fatigue parties began incorporating them into the second parallel, finishing the task soon after dawn. Cornwallis reported the loss of the works in a letter to Clinton, concluding: 'The safety of the place is, therefore, so precarious that I cannot recommend that the fleet and army should run any great risk in endeavouring to save us.'

Despite his pessimism, Cornwallis decided – or was persuaded – that it would be dishonourable to surrender without a sortie. At about 3:00am on 16 October, some 350 men (half from the Light Infantry, the rest from the Foot Guards and grenadier company of the 80th Foot) set out to cripple two batteries in the second parallel which, when completed, would threaten the Hornwork. Under Lt. Col. Abercrombie, they rushed out, drove off the guards and spiked four guns with bayonets, then moved left and spiked three more in an American battery, before some French infantry drove them off. The British lost eight dead and 12 prisoners, the French 20 killed and wounded and the Americans one man wounded

Although the bravery and dash of the British matched that of their foes, the result did not. Six hours later the guns were back in action, their fire forcing Cornwallis to consider one last escape attempt.

CORNWALLIS SURRENDERS

Throughout the war (since Boston, in fact) both sides felt that Nature favoured the Americans, and the siege of Yorktown was no exception. On the evening of 16 October, Tarleton sent over 16 boats, each capable of holding 100 men. Dividing his force into three groups, Cornwallis prepared to abandon Yorktown, leaving the 76th and the Anspachers as a sacrificial rearguard. Around 11:00pm, Cornwallis's first wave, 1,000 men of the Guards and Light Infantry, reached Gloucester between midnight and 1:00am, but a storm prevented further crossings until 2:00am. By then, it was too late for Yorke's brigade to cross without exposing Dundas to a dawn attack. Reluctantly, Cornwallis recalled the first group, which arrived back at 6:00am.

As dawn broke, the American and French batteries re-commenced their deadly work, with over 100 guns firing into the town. Just before 10:00am, a drummer in a red coat mounted the British parapet. The noise prevented anyone hearing him, but as the firing slackened, he was joined by an officer waving a white handkerchief, who approached the Allied lines. Blindfolded, he entered the Allied lines to deliver a sealed letter from Cornwallis, proposing a 24-hour truce so that terms of surrender could be discussed.

TOP AND CENTRE **Redoubt No. 9. These views show the front and rear of the redoubt, as reconstructed by the Colonial National Historical Park services. Note the steep sides, the entrance (just to the right of centre in the rear view), and the five-foot ditch surrounding the work. The people in the rear view give an idea of the size of the work, which covered the rising ground south-east of the town and a track leading up from the Moore House. (Author's photograph)**

RIGHT **The remains of Redoubt No. 10. Redoubt No. 10 was a small, square earthwork, sited just on a small rise at the edge of the cliffs to the south-east of Yorktown, to cover the beach. Sadly, 200 years of wind and water erosion means that little of the work remains, and what there is must be fenced off to protect it and the public. The metal fencing approximates to the position of the 'fraise' or palisade placed in the ditches around all the British works to further impede any attacker. (Author's photograph)**

LEFT **The Second Parallel. Once the two redoubts were in Allied hands, working parties raced forward to incorporate them into the Second Parallel. This battery mounted six 18-pdr. and 24-pdr. guns (though not on the naval-style carriages shown) and two howitzers, as well as several mortars. (Author's photographs)**

A view of Yorktown from Gloucester. This painting, supposedly drawn by one of Simcoe's officers, gives an idea of how the Gloucester garrison saw the siege. Note the wooden stockade, left. Strangely, the ship in the centre seems to be flying a Dutch or French tricolour; unless it is a captured vessel, this may suggest that the painting was begun, or completed, after the siege. (Courtesy: Colonial Williamsburg)

Washington agreed to suspend hostilities for two hours; Cornwallis (who later claimed Washington had given him too little time) requested that his troops be paroled to Europe, not to serve against the Allies for the remainder of the war. Washington, aware that a relief force from Clinton could enter Chesapeake Bay at any time, replied that any surrender would involve the garrison becoming prisoners of war. Cornwallis agreed to discussions while seeking assurances for his own possessions and those of his officers, and free passage for Loyalists.

Each side sent two commissioners to the Moore House on 18 October. Around midnight, their efforts were sent to Washington for approval; he agreed that the garrison would march out to lay down their arms and colours; the cavalry could ride with drawn sabres; and all officers would be paroled. In addition, Cornwallis could use the *Bonetta* (which would not be searched) to return his possessions to New York. In retaliation for the humiliation of the Charleston garrison, the British could not play a French or American tune, and must keep their colours cased. The terms were agreed by Cornwallis, who signed the capitulation documents, as did Symonds, the senior Royal Navy officer. The documents were returned to the Allied lines, where they were also signed by Washington, Rochambeau and de Barras (for de Grasse).

At 2:00pm on 19 October 1781, Cornwallis's army marched out of Yorktown on the Hampton Road, past the French and Americans. The British pointedly looked front, acknowledging only the colours of the French regiments to their right. A French officer noted the 'very fine looking' grenadiers and strong Scots, but felt the English troops were small; the Germans displayed order and discipline, while the British were arrogant and haughty towards the Americans.

The column was led not by Cornwallis – who pleaded illness[10] – but by his deputy, O'Hara. Approaching the Allied commanders, O'Hara offered his sword to de Rochambeau, who courteously declined and pointed towards Washington, who in turn indicated his own second-in-

BELOW A View of Yorktown, by J Trumbull. This panoramic view shows the town and the ground to the south and south-east, and was made some years after the siege as a preliminary sketch for his famous painting of the surrender. The British works can still be seen; those of the besiegers were levelled immediately after the siege, as Washington feared they might be used by Clinton to besiege the Allies. The large building is probably Nelson's house, just inside the Hornwork. (Courtesy: Frick Art Reference Library, New York)

THE SIEGE OF YORKTOWN
1-19 OCTOBER 1781

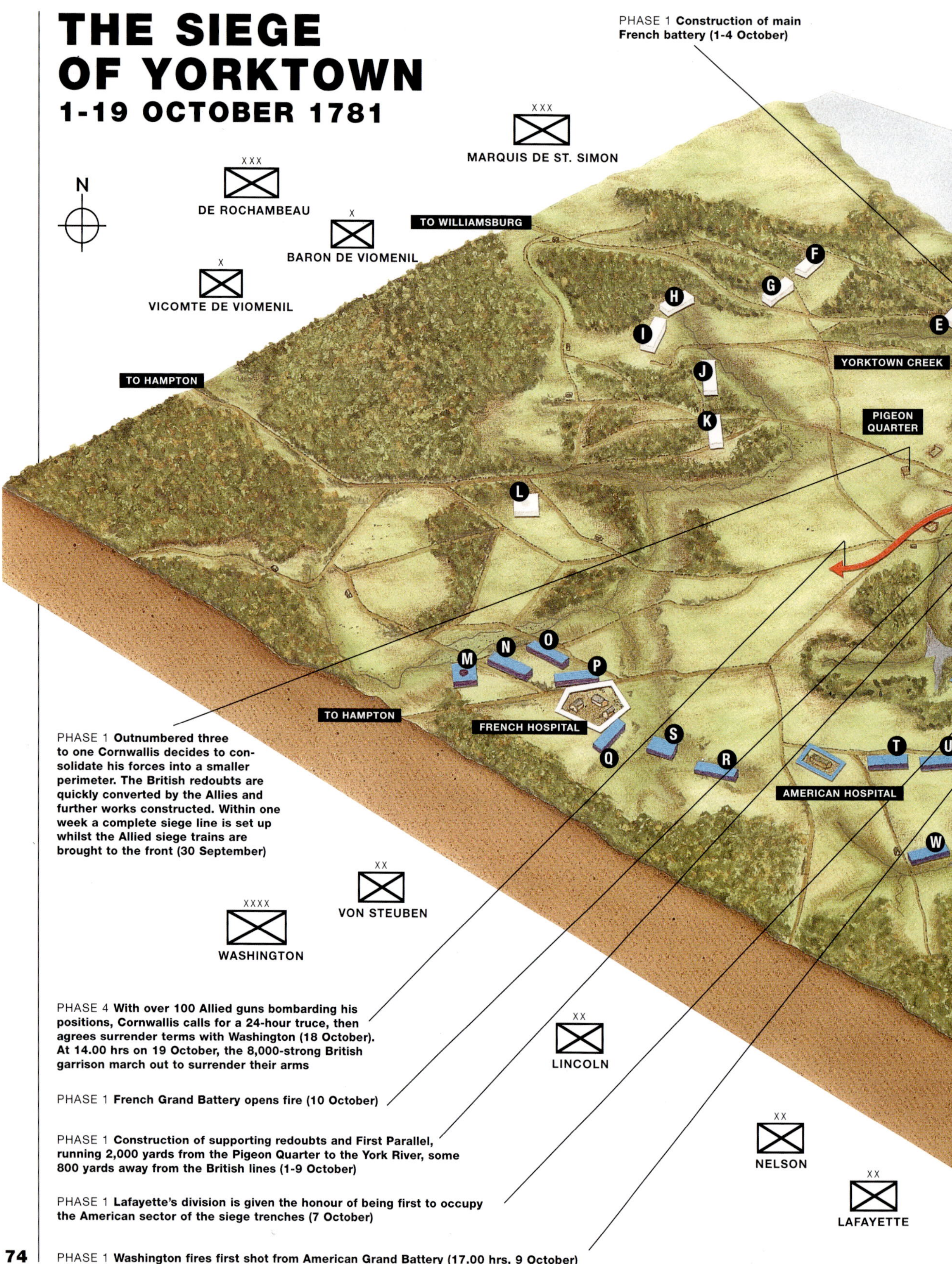

PHASE 1 **Construction of main French battery (1-4 October)**

PHASE 1 **Outnumbered three to one Cornwallis decides to consolidate his forces into a smaller perimeter. The British redoubts are quickly converted by the Allies and further works constructed. Within one week a complete siege line is set up whilst the Allied siege trains are brought to the front (30 September)**

PHASE 4 **With over 100 Allied guns bombarding his positions, Cornwallis calls for a 24-hour truce, then agrees surrender terms with Washington (18 October). At 14.00 hrs on 19 October, the 8,000-strong British garrison march out to surrender their arms**

PHASE 1 **French Grand Battery opens fire (10 October)**

PHASE 1 **Construction of supporting redoubts and First Parallel, running 2,000 yards from the Pigeon Quarter to the York River, some 800 yards away from the British lines (1-9 October)**

PHASE 1 **Lafayette's division is given the honour of being first to occupy the American sector of the siege trenches (7 October)**

PHASE 1 **Washington fires first shot from American Grand Battery (17.00 hrs, 9 October)**

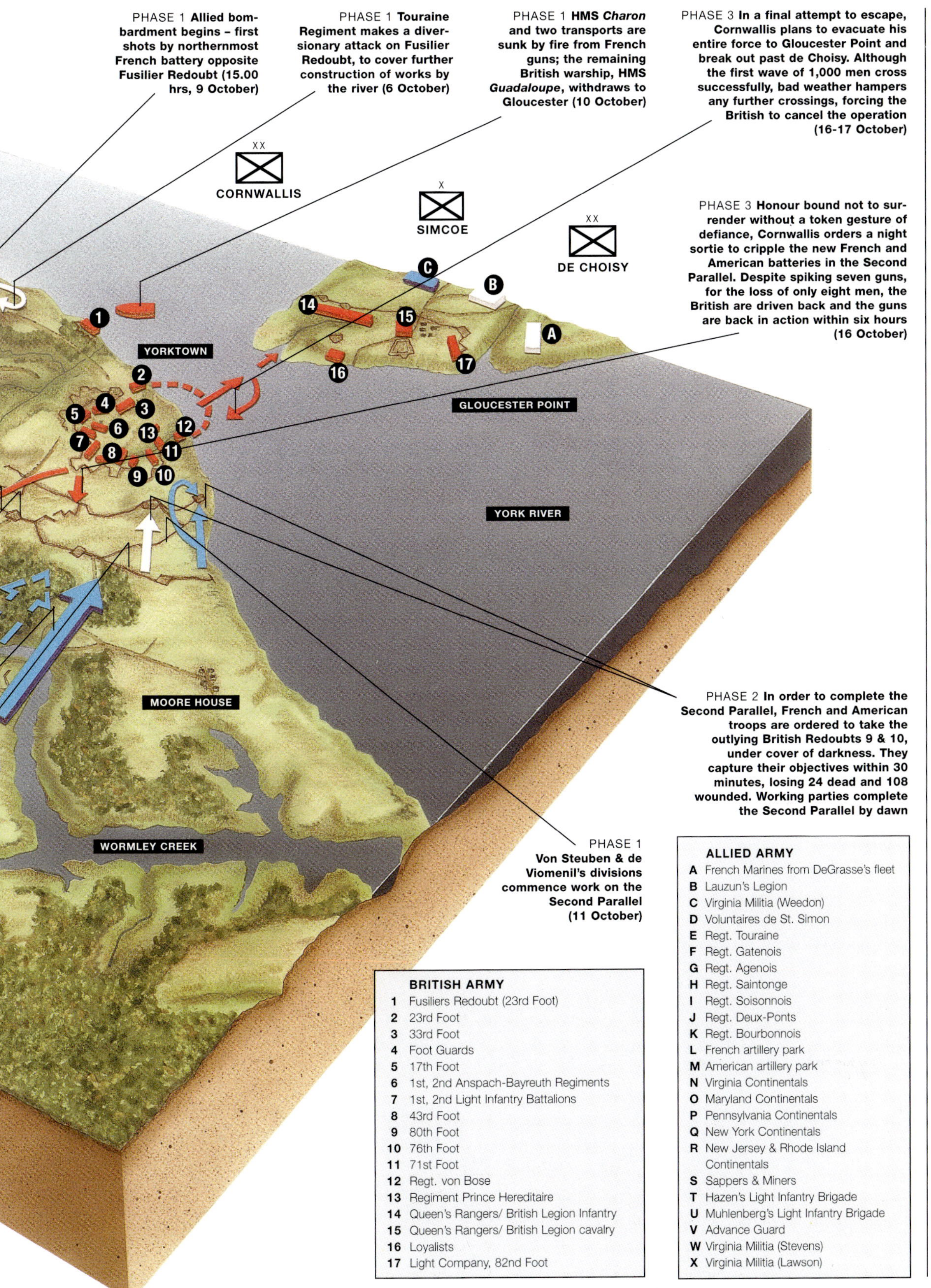
PHASE 1 **Allied bombardment begins – first shots by northernmost French battery opposite Fusilier Redoubt (15.00 hrs, 9 October)**
PHASE 1 **Touraine Regiment makes a diversionary attack on Fusilier Redoubt, to cover further construction of works by the river (6 October)**
PHASE 1 **HMS *Charon* and two transports are sunk by fire from French guns; the remaining British warship, HMS *Guadaloupe*, withdraws to Gloucester (10 October)**
PHASE 3 **In a final attempt to escape, Cornwallis plans to evacuate his entire force to Gloucester Point and break out past de Choisy. Although the first wave of 1,000 men cross successfully, bad weather hampers any further crossings, forcing the British to cancel the operation (16-17 October)**
XX
CORNWALLIS
X
SIMCOE
XX
DE CHOISY
PHASE 3 **Honour bound not to surrender without a token gesture of defiance, Cornwallis orders a night sortie to cripple the new French and American batteries in the Second Parallel. Despite spiking seven guns, for the loss of only eight men, the British are driven back and the guns are back in action within six hours (16 October)**
YORKTOWN
GLOUCESTER POINT
YORK RIVER
MOORE HOUSE
WORMLEY CREEK
PHASE 2 **In order to complete the Second Parallel, French and American troops are ordered to take the outlying British Redoubts 9 & 10, under cover of darkness. They capture their objectives within 30 minutes, losing 24 dead and 108 wounded. Working parties complete the Second Parallel by dawn**
PHASE 1 **Von Steuben & de Viomenil's divisions commence work on the Second Parallel (11 October)**
BRITISH ARMY
1 Fusiliers Redoubt (23rd Foot)
2 23rd Foot
3 33rd Foot
4 Foot Guards
5 17th Foot
6 1st, 2nd Anspach-Bayreuth Regiments
7 1st, 2nd Light Infantry Battalions
8 43rd Foot
9 80th Foot
10 76th Foot
11 71st Foot
12 Regt. von Bose
13 Regiment Prince Hereditaire
14 Queen's Rangers/ British Legion Infantry
15 Queen's Rangers/ British Legion cavalry
16 Loyalists
17 Light Company, 82nd Foot
ALLIED ARMY
A French Marines from DeGrasse's fleet
B Lauzun's Legion
C Virginia Militia (Weedon)
D Voluntaires de St. Simon
E Regt. Touraine
F Regt. Gatenois
G Regt. Agenois
H Regt. Saintonge
I Regt. Soisonnois
J Regt. Deux-Ponts
K Regt. Bourbonnois
L French artillery park
M American artillery park
N Virginia Continentals
O Maryland Continentals
P Pennsylvania Continentals
Q New York Continentals
R New Jersey & Rhode Island Continentals
S Sappers & Miners
T Hazen's Light Infantry Brigade
U Muhlenberg's Light Infantry Brigade
V Advance Guard
W Virginia Militia (Stevens)
X Virginia Militia (Lawson)

LEFT **The Augustine Moore House. Here, the commissioners appointed by Cornwallis and Washington formulated the articles of surrender, on 18 October. (Author's photograph)**

command, Lincoln. As this cameo was played out, the former garrison of Yorktown, including the cavalry from Gloucester, were laying down their weapons and accoutrements in a nearby field, watched by a circle of Lauzun's cavalry. The rest of the Gloucester garrison surrendered to de Choisy the following day.

In all, 7,247 troops surrendered, along with 840 naval personnel[11]; 309 defenders had perished – many from sickness – and 44 had deserted.

BELOW ***The Surrender at Yorktown*****, by J Trumbull. In all of his historical tableaux, Trumbull's aim was to illustrate the *dramatis personae* rather than record any specific event. This work encompasses the entire Allied high command, principally Lincoln accepting the British surrender from O'Hara, watched by from right to left, Hamilton (standing nearest centre); von Steuben, Lafayette and Knox (mounted, under the American flag); Washington (to right of Lincoln). On the French side are Rochambeau (left centre, on prancing horse); his four marechaux-de-camp; the Duc de Lauzun, and the Comte de Deux-Ponts (extreme left, dismounted). (Courtesy: Yale University Art Gallery,Cambridge)**

The British handed over to the victorious Allied besieging force 243 pieces of artillery with over 2,000 rounds of ammunition, 8,000 muskets and 266,000 cartridges, 2,000 swords and 100 flags (including six British and 18 German regimental colours). In addition, there were 300 horses (hundreds more had been slaughtered during the siege because of lack of space and forage), 43 wagons and – most surprisingly – massive quantities of food albeit of indifferent quality: 100,000 pounds of meat, 73,000 pounds of flour, 66,000 pounds of bread and 20,000 pounds of butter, as well as large stocks of oatmeal, peas, sugar, rice, cocoa, coffee and various types of alcohol.

The British and German rank-and-file marched off to Williamsburg, then to prisons in Virginia and Maryland. The officers (less 180 who remained with the men to keep order) were allowed to sail to any British-held port, but under the terms of their parole could take no further part in the war until officially 'exchanged'.

Washington kept his promise to hang every deserter found in Yorktown, but celebrated the victory by releasing all American soldiers imprisoned for disciplinary offences. Having sent his aide-de-camp, Tench Tilghman, to Philadelphia to present his victory despatch to Congress, he wrote to Maj. Gen. Heath at New York, saying, with masterly understatement, that: 'we may have underestimated the importance of the naval campaign'.

The British campaign to re-conquer the South had finally been extinguished, and with the loss of Yorktown, went their chances of winning the war.

BELOW ***The Surrender at Yorktown*, by J Trumbull. The meticulous Trumbull invariably made preliminary pencil sketches of individuals, then grouped them in oil sketches such as this. Here Lincoln and O'Hara are bareheaded (as they would most likely have been at such a moment). Other interesting detail omitted from the final work are the French grenadier officer (left) and the more unusual version of the 'stars and stripes', with red, white and blue bands. (Courtesy, Detroit Institute of Fine Arts)**

AFTERMATH

On 24 October Graves and Hood arrived off the Capes with a British fleet of 36 ships carrying Clinton and 7,000 men. Despite picking up escapees from Yorktown, and meeting HMS *Nymphe* carrying Cornwallis's dispatch of 15 October (recommending that no relief attempt be made), they refused to believe the Earl had surrendered. They waited five days, during which time another eight ships arrived, but when a frigate reported 45 enemy sail in Hampton Roads, Graves decided – against the wishes of Hood and Clinton – to return to New York, effectively ending the Yorktown campaign.

Meanwhile in Yorktown, with the surrender formalities complete, 'Old World' courtesies took over, and French and British officers entertained each other in some luxury (Rochambeau even lent Cornwallis £150,000 to allow him and his staff to return French hospitality). All this seemed strange, even insulting, to the Americans, who felt snubbed not only by their captives, but even by their own allies. With few men – or officers – boasting proper uniforms, and with pay months in arrears (Tilghman was so poor he had to be fed and housed by Congressmen when he fell ill), the Americans found themselves looking on, as the 'professionals' fraternised.

At the beginning of November, Washington suggested that the Allies attack Savannah and Charleston to remove the British presence from the South completely. However, de Grasse, who had a secret agreement with the Spanish to winter in the Caribbean, insisted on sailing for the West Indies before the weather turned. Having ordered the Allied siege lines levelled to prevent the British using them in the future, a disappointed Washington returned to New York with his army (less a small detachment of Continentals sent to reinforce Greene), while Rochambeau's troops remained in Virginia for the winter.

THE RIPPLES SPREAD

On 25 November news reached Germain of the surrender, confirmed by letter from Clinton. He immediately told North, who replied: 'Oh, God! It is all over!' Although 30,000 British troops remained in North America, a mounting national debt and fears of a Franco-Spanish invasion of Great Britain destroyed the will to continue. Germain, taking the brunt of Opposition fury, resigned in February 1782, and in March, North's government lost a general election. Despite his threat to abdicate rather than give up the American colonies, George III was forced to accept peace and their independence as pre-conditions of the Whigs forming a new government.

Although Rodney had defeated de Grasse at the Saintes in April,

Germain's successor, Lord Shelburne, was sent to Paris to meet the American peace commissioners. In America, Sir Guy Carleton succeeded Clinton as commander-in-chief in America, with orders to take no offensive action, but to plan a total evacuation. Apart from some skirmishing on the western frontier and in the South, where Greene was besieging Charleston, the fighting was effectively over.

THE ROAD TO PEACE

During a summer of negotiation, it became clear that the French agenda involved supporting Spanish, rather than American, interests; indeed, the Spanish seemed more hostile to American independence than the British. As the French tried to negotiate a secret peace with Great Britain, the American delegates asked the British to tacitly recognise American independence by negotiating with 'the 13 United States' – a price the British happily paid to end the Franco-American alliance. A preliminary agreement was reached in November 1782, which would eventually form the principal terms of the final treaty.

By December 1782, the British had evacuated Savannah and Charleston, and Rochambeau's army was heading for the West Indies via Boston. For the Americans, however, the problems of self-governance were just beginning, with fierce arguments for either a strong central government or a loose confederation of states. The army, too, seethed with discontent over pay, and officers circulated pamphlets threatening Congress and refusing to fight if hostilities recommenced, unless the debts were settled. (Ironically, Congress could not raise the money because individual states refused to levy taxes.)

Eventually, the enlisted men were discharged with undated promissory notes for three months' pay (which would not be redeemed for years, and then only as land grants) and permission to retain their muskets. A rump of active units were left watching the British in New York, under Washington's immediate command.

The final peace treaty was signed in September 1783, and two months later (a year to the day after the news of Yorktown reached London), the last British troops left New York. The evacuation of the former colonies had taken a total of 100,000 Loyalists to Canada or Great Britain, and a royal commission eventually awarded over £3,000,000 in compensation to those who had lost all serving their King.

Having already said good-bye to the army in his final General Order of 18 October, Washington bade farewell to his staff at an emotional dinner in December and appeared before Congress to hand back his commission as commander-in-chief. The war for American independence was over; the struggle for American nationhood was about to begin.

Washington and his generals at Yorktown, by C W Peale. Washington (second from left) surveys the York River, with Lafayette (at left), Rochambeau (third from right) and others, apparently standing behind the Fusilier Redoubt, with Yorktown Creek just below them. However, though the artist clearly intended to depict Yorktown, the ambiguous presence of a windmill, and the orientation of the shadows, actually suggest Gloucester Point is the more likely location. (Courtesy: Colonial Williamsburg)

THE BATTLEFIELD TODAY

It is still possible to follow the routes taken by Cornwallis and Lafayette through central and eastern Virginia in 1781, but most of the minor battle sites are now built up, farmed, or overgrown. However, the Yorktown battlefield – or at least the main part of it – has been preserved (Gloucester Point now lies buried under the Colemen Memorial Bridge). The town and the reconstructed siege lines are now part of the Colonial National Historical Park, which includes Jamestown, the first English settlement in the New World; Colonial Williamsburg, which is worth a full day's visit for its restored period buildings and 'living history' displays; and Green Spring (four miles south-west of Williamsburg, via State Highway 31 south-west, then west on State 5). While it is possible to 'walk' Yorktown and its defences – and even the surrounding parallels – a full tour, covering the Allied camps, requires a car.

For Yorktown, take the Colonial Parkway (which covers the entire National Park) from Williamsburg north-east to Yorktown, a drive of about 13 miles. A narrow spur onto State 238 leads past the 'Yorktown Victory Center', which includes a reconstruction of an American camp manned by local re-enactors; a cinema showing 'The Road to Yorktown'; an historical tour outlining the events leading to the Revolution, ending in a small museum, full of local, as well as military, artefacts; and a souvenir shop with a good selection of books. The background information provided, and the opening times, make this a good starting point for any tour of Yorktown.

North of the Center, a field overlooking the river contains the remains of the Fusilier Redoubt, which held out until the end of the siege; the rest has disappeared through erosion of the cliff, but the general form of the work is visible. (It is deliberate policy to allow the

Re-enactors' encampment, Yorktown Victory Centre. The centre, which includes 'living history' displays and a museum, is just off the Colonial Parkway route into Yorktown (opposite the Fusilier Redoubt). It shows how an American unit's camp would have looked in the woods to the south of Yorktown, behind the First Parallel. (Author's photographs)

grass to grow long around the earthworks, as it prevents erosion by the weather – and the tourists.)

From the redoubt, head south-east along Water Street and park the car (Yorktown itself is best seen on foot). On Water Street are the caves Cornwallis reputedly used as his headquarters (it actually housed other officers), and the Archer cottage, the only waterfront building to survive both the siege and a major fire in 1814; some piling from the Town Wharf can also be seen at low water.

At the south-west end of de Grasse Street is the Victory Monument,

ABOVE **Farm buildings. Although located inside Yorktown, this group of buildings is typical of the plantation outbuildings dotted around the surrounding area. These farms and slave quarters were used by the besiegers as hospitals, arsenals and unit headquarters. (Author's photographs)**

LEFT AND BELOW **Cornwallis's Cave and the Archer House. Though legend claims that the cave was the British commander's headquarters during the siege, it was in fact used by other officers, and as a shelter for civilians. (Author's photographs)**

ABOVE **The Grace Church. The church survived not only the siege of 1781, but another in 1862, and a fire that devastated Yorktown itself in 1814. (Author's photograph)**

The Digges House. Built in 1760; one of the few frame-built homes to survive the siege. (Author's photograph)

and Zweibrucken Road containing the foundations of Secretary Nelson's house and the Hornwork, which covered the Hampton Road entrance to the town. From the latter (enlarged by the Confederates during the Civil War), the visitor can note the gently undulating ground around Yorktown, despite the woods.

Heading back along Main Street, several buildings remain from the siege, including Thomas Sessions' house (the oldest building in

The Custom House. This, the oldest customs house in the US. It is owned and maintained by the "Comte de Grasse" Chapter of the Daughters of the Revolution. (Author's photograph)

Yorktown), Governor Nelson's House (the sole survivor of three Nelson residences), the 'Custom House', and the Grace Church, built in 1697, where several of the Nelson family are buried. Several lanes lead west to modern, private homes, and it is possible to see the outline of the western defences about half-way down these tracks. Facing east, the Great Valley is one of the few natural 'washes' between the cliffs to the waterfront (another is Tobacco Road, by the Victory Monument).

South-east of the town is the Visitor Center, with a museum that has one of Washington's tents and a reconstruction of HMS *Charon* (housing naval artefacts recovered from the river), as well as a cinema and a south-facing observation deck, overlooking the British defences. The main British line was altered and enlarged during a later siege in 1862 (a Union cemetery from this time stands just behind the Allied lines), so these works are not as they were in 1781. However, the Allied lines, which were levelled after the siege on Washington's orders, and the British outer defences, were reconstructed in the 1930s for the 150th anniversary celebrations.

Redoubt No. 9 is restored and can be visited, but redoubt No. 10 has suffered from coastal erosion and the remains are fenced off. Near them lies the second American 'grand battery', some 300 yards from the British main line. Much of the first parallel, some 6-700 yards further back, is covered by woods on the American flank, but the French part, west of the Hampton road, is visible. The French 'grand battery' has been reconstructed, including contemporary ordnance, and to the west

ABOVE AND TOP **Views of the Allied Lines. These views are from the observation deck of the Yorktown Visitor Center (situated between the sites of Redoubts No.s 6 and 7), looking south and south-east (respectively). The top photograph shows Redoubt No. 9 some 2-300 yards straight ahead and the second parallel American Grand Battery to the left. The second photo shows the first parallel American Grand Battery in the middle distance; the French Grand Battery is hidden by the trees in the right foreground. (Author's photographs)**

of the road that runs by the battery is a redoubt built to extend the abandoned British outer line.

Outside Yorktown, two 'tours' – some 16-17 miles in all – cover the rest of the area. The 'red' tour covers the siege itself (including the southern defences), and takes in the Moore House, a mile south-east of the town. It then heads west through Lafayette's camp and the American hospital to the Surrender Field, which has a viewing platform surrounded by captured British ordnance.

The 'yellow' tour begins at the Surrender Field and covers the remaining American – and all of the French – encampments, headquarters and artillery parks. There is little to see beyond commemorative plaques and clearings in dense woods, but the tour gives some idea of the terrain and the distances that the French, especially, had to cover to take their positions in the trenches. On the return leg to Yorktown, the route passes between two surviving British redoubts in the Pigeon Quarter, although the view that their occupants might have 'enjoyed' in 1781 is now obscured by woods.

Outside Yorktown, other places of interest include the excellent Mariners' Museum at Newport News (with a large section on Nelson and the Napoleonic wars), and the US Navy yards at Norfolk and Portsmouth. Head south from Yorktown on US Highway 17, then Morris Boulevard to Interstate 64. (For those with a thirst for more than knowledge, there is also a large brewery on US Highway 60, heading north from Hampton to Williamsburg.)

ABOVE **Gloucester Point, from the beach at Yorktown. Subsequent development, especially the construction of the Colemen Memorial Bridge, have removed virtually all trace of the siege on that side of the river, but the photo does give an idea of the distance. (Author's photograph)**

LEFT **The Victory Monument. Although authorised by Congress in 1781, work on the main shaft did not begin until the centennial celebrations of 1881; the monument was completed three years later. The original 'Liberty' was hit by lightning in 1942, and the present figure replaced her in 1956. (Author's photograph)**

CHRONOLOGY

THE COURSE OF THE WAR 1775-1781

19 April 1775 – Lexington and Concord
April 1775 to March 1776 – Siege of Boston
May 1775 to October 1776 – American attack on Canada
4 July 1776 – Declaration of Independence
July to December 1776 – New York campaign
December 1776 to January 1777 – Trenton and Princeton
June to October 1777 – Saratoga campaign
July to November 1777 – Philadelphia campaign
December 1777 to March 1778 – Valley Forge
6 February 1778 – Franco-American alliance signed
8 May 1778 – Clinton replaces Howe as commander-in-chief
June 1778 – British leave Philadelphia for New York
July to August 1778 – Allies attack Newport, Rhode Island
July to November 1778 – Loyalist/Indian campaign in north
December 1778 to January 1779 – British capture Georgia
January to October 1779 – Allies besiege Savannah
8 May 1779 – Spain declares war on Britain
28 February 1780 – League of Armed Neutrality formed
June to August 1780 – British campaign in South Carolina
July 1780 – French forces arrive at Newport, Rhode Island
25 September 1780 – Arnold defects to the British
September to December 1780 – South Carolina campaign
January to March 1781 – North Carolina campaign
20 December 1780 – Britain declares war against Holland

THE WAR IN VIRGINIA 1775-1780

23 March 1775 – 'Give me liberty, or give me death' speech by Patrick Henry at second Virginia Convention
8 June – Governor Dunmore flees to HMS *Fowey*
15 June – Washington offered command of Continental Army
15 July – First Virginian troops leave for Boston
12 October – 14th Foot raid areas around Norfolk
7 November – Dunmore's Emancipation Proclamation
15 November – British foil ambush at Kemp's Landing
9 December – British defeated at Great Bridge
1 January 1776 – British bombard Norfolk; Continentals riot
6 February – Americans burn and abandon Norfolk
18 December – British merchants ordered to leave Virginia
20 July 1777 – Treaty ends war between Virginia and Cherokees
10 December – Clark presents plan to capture Detroit
22 January 1778 – Loyalists' estates sequestrated
4 July – Clark captures Kaskaskia and Vincennes
17 December – British recapture Vincennes
16 January 1779 – Saratoga prisoners arrive at Charlottesville
24 February – Clark retakes Vincennes
10 April – Shelby attacks remaining Cherokee in Tennessee
8 May – British attack Portsmouth and Suffolk
23 June – All Loyalist-owned land confiscated
30 November – Meat and grain exports banned
7 April 1780 – Capital moved from Williamsburg to Richmond
12–29 May – Virginia Line lost at Charleston and Waxhaws
10 June – Compulsory purchase of all excess foodstuffs
20 October – Leslie arrives in Hampton Roads
20 November – Von Steuben made Virginia Continental commander
30 December – Arnold arrives in Chesapeake Bay

THE FINAL CAMPAIGN JANUARY TO OCTOBER 1781

5 January – Arnold attacks and burns Richmond
22 January – Clark leaves Richmond to attack Detroit
14 March – Lafayette lands at Yorktown
15 March – Cornwallis commences march to Virginia
16 March – Naval action off the Virginia Capes
26 March – Phillips arrives in Virginia
18–30 April – British raids
9 May 1781 – Spanish capture Pensacola, Florida
12 May 1781 – Cornwallis enters Virginia
13 May – Phillips dies and Arnold resumes command
20–24 May – Cornwallis joins Arnold at Petersburg
3–4 June – Raids by Simcoe and Tarleton
5 June – Point of Fork
10 June – Von Steuben and Wayne reinforce Lafayette
26 June – Skirmish at Spencer's Ordinary
6 July – Battle of Green Spring
9–24 July – Tarleton's raids in western Virginia
14 July – Cornwallis reaches Portsmouth
19 August – Washington and Rochambeau leave Newport
31 August – De Grasse arrives in Chesapeake Bay
5 September – Battle of the Chesapeake

10 September – De Barras arrives with the Allied siege train
14 September – Washington and Rochambeau reach Williamsburg
26 September – Allied troops assemble in Williamsburg
28 September – The Allies march to Yorktown
30 September – Cornwallis abandons outer defences
1 October – Allies prepare to besiege Yorktown
3 October – Tarleton and Lauzun clash near Gloucester
6 October – The Allies begin work on the first parallel; French diversionary attack on the Fusilier Redoubt
7 October – Lafayette's men enter the trenches
9 October – French and American batteries open fire
10 October – HMS *Charon* set on fire
11 October – Second parallel opened
14 October – Night attacks on Redoubts 9 and 10
15 October – Second parallel completed (morning); Abercrombie's detachment attacks Allied batteries (night)
16 October – Unsuccessful attempt to escape to Gloucester
17 October – Cornwallis requests cessation of hostilities
18 October – Commissioners discuss surrender terms
19 October – British surrender
23 October – Loyalists escape on the *Bonetta*
25 October – Clinton's relief force reaches Chesapeake
4 November – Cornwallis leaves Yorktown on the *Cochrane*
19 November – Cornwallis arrives in New York

THE ROAD TO PEACE JANUARY 1782 TO DECEMBER 1783

23 February 1782 – Carleton replaces Clinton
March to August – Frontier war continues
12 April – Rodney defeats de Grasse at the Saintes
11 July – British abandon Savannah
30 November – First peace treaty signed in Paris
14 December – British evacuate Charleston
19 April 1783 – Congress proclaims end to hostilities
3 September – Final peace treaty signed
25 November – Main British evacuation of New York
23 December – Washington retires as commander-in-chief

***Siege of Yorktown*, by L van Blarenberghe.**
The artist was reputedly an eye-witness, and his paintings of the siege and the surrender include much valuable detail. Here, a French regiment in column of platoons passes one of the abandoned British outer redoubts on its way to the trenches, reducing to single file on entering the covered way in the middle distance. The abandoned first parallel is visible, with the second parallel and British defences shrouded in smoke; redoubts 9 and 10 are to the right of centre and the black dot just above the horizon is a falling British shell (from which the horsemen are taking cover). (Courtesy: Musée de Versailles, Paris, & Colonial Williamsburg)

A GUIDE TO FURTHER READING

The remarks in the corresponding chapter of *Boston 1775* (Campaign 37) about history being written by the winners, applies equally here. Any works – including those listed below – should be read with care, regardless of origin (British writers also tend to have a 'hidden agenda'). Readers are also directed to the bibliography in *Boston 1775* with regard to the causes of the war, and the opposing forces.

On the opposing commanders: Wickwire, F. and M., *Cornwallis and the War of Independence*, London, 1971; and Flexner, J., *Washington*, London, 1973 (a one-volume version of his four-volume epic). For details on the other main characters, see Boatner, M., *Biographical Dictionary of the American War of Independence*, London, 1974; and *Dictionary of National Biography*, London 1901.

On the opposing armies, Chartrand, R., *The French Army in the American War of Independence*, Osprey, 1991. Other useful works include: Frey, S., *The British soldier in America*, University of Texas, 1981; Dohla, J, *A Hessian diary of the American Revolution*, University of Oklahoma, 1990, (mainly covering the Virginia campaign and his subsequent captivity); Bonsal, S., *When the French were here*, New York, 1968; and Balch, T., *The French in America during the War of Independence*, Boston, 1972. Van Doren, C., *Mutiny in January*, New York, 1943, covers the mutiny of the Pennsylvania Line and its effect on the war.

On the war in Virginia, Selby, J., *A Chronology of Virginia in the War of Independence*, University of Virginia, 1973; and Eckenrode, H., *The Revolution in Virginia*, Hampton, 1964. For the Virginia campaign and siege of Yorktown, Fleming T., *The Battle of Yorktown*, New York, 1968; Johnston, H., *The Yorktown Campaign and the surrender of Cornwallis*, New York, 1981 (written for the centennial, and with useful statistics); and Davis, B., *The campaign that won America*, New York, 1989.

On the naval campaign, Syrett, D., *The Royal Navy in American Waters*, Aldershot, 1989, analyses British naval policy and actions; and Mahan, A.T., *The Influence of Sea Power upon History*, reprinted, New York, 1987, and *Major Operations of the Navies in the American War of Independence*, New Jersey, 1913, give an interesting American perspective on 18th-century naval strategy (unfettered by preconceptions about Britannia ruling the waves).

For maps and charts: Marshall, W., and Peckham, H., *Campaigns of the American Revolution*, New Jersey, 1976; and Symonds, C., and Clipson, W., *A Battlefield Atlas of the American Revolution*, Annapolis, 1986.

Finally, two booklets indispensable to wargamers and order of battle researchers: Novak, G., *We have always governed ourselves*, and *Rise and fight again*, *Champaign* (Illinois), 1990 and 1993; a year–by–year account of how the armies were organised (and re–organised), including scarce data on strengths and *ad hoc* units.

WARGAMING THE YORKTOWN CAMPAIGN

The comments in the corresponding chapter of *Boston 1775* (Campaign 37), on the popularity of the War of Independence among wargamers, also just as relevant here. The enduring mythology of American patriotic fervour conquering any and every hardship – aided and abetted by British incompetence – suggests that any historical simulation of Yorktown offers nothing but a brief, one-sided siege. However, if the entrapment of Cornwallis is seen as merely the final act in a campaign fought across the length and breadth of Virginia – and in the waters off its coast – some interesting games can be played.

It is worth noting that here, as so often in this war, the armies – and regiments – were usually small, so the tabletop general can command a wide range of colourful, specialised units, capable of operating independently. The figure gamer can also use very low figure/man ratios without going to excessive expense, creating units that not only look more realistic on the table, but which also need some thought as to the space and time required for manoeuvre – as with the real thing.

The Storming of Redoubt 10, by Eugene Lami. Although undoubtedly capturing the dash of the American assault of 14/15 October, this painting contains several inaccuracies. The attack is in daylight; the redoubt is far too big; the entrance was at the rear, not facing the American lines; and both sides wear 1790s uniforms. (Courtesy: Virginia State Library, Richmond)

The nature of the forces involved also requires a rethink of rules, whether for tabletop or board games. The '+1 for being British' approach does not work here – arguably, most of the enemy are also 'British' (at least until 1783) – and the success of the night assaults during the siege of Yorktown (especially that of the French, which was quite heavily opposed) suggests high morale and competence among the Allies generally. For both figure and board games, victory conditions should be loaded – possibly by deducting points according to percentage casualties suffered – to reflect the paralysis of 'Pyrrhic' victories and promote greater caution, even in one-off games.

TOBACCO RAIDS

The early days of the rebellion in Virginia offer a fascinating campaign game. Although it is impossible for the British player to crush the rebellion, internal dissension and sensitive egos in the American camp allowed Dunmore to do much with very little; only the defeat at Great Bridge gave the Americans time to consolidate and force him to seek an alternative base. With his small fleet, core of Regulars and growing numbers of disaffected whites and escaped slaves, the British player can cause considerable damage and tie down large numbers of militia.

As the British came to appreciate the value of Virginia to the American war effort, it acquired a more prominent – albeit flawed – position in their overall strategy. Both the

BRITISH NIGHT ATTACK, 16 OCTOBER 1781

After capturing the two redoubts, the Allies completed the second parallel, including two batteries capable of enfilading the British defences. At 3.00am on 16 October, 350 volunteers under Lt.-Col. Robert Aber-crombie, left the Hornwork, aiming for the junction between the French and American forces. Arriving at the two newly-built batteries, they found no working parties. Pretending to be Americans, they headed west, surprising a detachment of the Agenais

Mathew/Collier and Arnold/ Phillips raids can be re-created using the actual orders-of-battle, timetables and objectives (particularly value of material destroyed) to calculate success or failure. If the player(s) control the British forces, with the opposition pre-programmed or controlled by the umpire, there is an opportunity for 'role-playing', as well as figure-gaming. Players would use their ingenuity to locate and destroy American magazines, capture senior military and political personages, and attempt to raise recruits. However, there is always the possibility of the raiders straying too far from their escape route – the naval transports - and being trapped by unexpected concentrations of militia.

For Arnold's raid, various 'what ifs' can be thrown in (generated either by die-roll, or a malicious umpire), such as the co-ordinated arrival of Lafayette, the French force from Newport, and local militia. An interesting two-player role-playing game might follow a successful attempt to capture or kill Arnold, giving Simcoe and Dundas the opportunity to exercise their 'dormant commissions'.

regiment guarding a French battery, killing one soldier and wounding six officers and 37 men. Spiking four guns with bayonets, they continued into an American battery, where they were challenged. The British spiked three more guns and inflicted 17 casualties, before a party of French grenadiers led by Lafayette's brother-in-law drove them back to their own lines. However, the efforts of Abercrombie's men were to no avail – within six hours, all the spiked guns were back in action. (Adam Hook)

CHASING LAFAYETTE

The summer campaign between Lafayette and Cornwallis provides a rare opportunity to fight AWI battles between armies of comparable strength and quality. Lafayette's Continentals should be the equal of Cornwallis's best units – possibly even superior to newly-raised units, such as the 76th and 80th – and even the militia had comparatively good combat records. The British superiority in mounted troops was matched by the local knowledge of their opponents and the latter's ability to gather in extra militia as and when needed.

Two particularly colourful games could be created from Tarleton's raid on Charlottesville and near-capture of the Virginia legislature, and Simcoe's march to Point-of-Fork and the action against von Steuben's militia. Tarleton's force, especially, was unusual in consisting entirely of mounted troops, while Simcoe's raid provides opportunities for the wily gamer to incorporate all sorts of ruses and stratagems – such as the capture of enemy cavalry and use of their uniforms – to conceal his approach and true strength.

The main action, at Green Spring Farm, would need careful umpiring to re-create in its entirety, balancing Lafayette's caution against the surprise undoubtedly achieved by Cornwallis. One option would be to game the preliminary skirmishing of Tarleton's cavalry and the British picket company with Wayne's advance guard of dragoons, mounted riflemen and light infantry, victory being determined by the length of time the British can hold off their opponents. This game would be very much of the 'skirmish' variety, and could be refought at a 1:1 figure/man ratio. Another option would be to recreate the moment when the British emerged from the woods by the James River to confront Wayne's reinforced brigade, and see whether the historical tactics can save the day for the Americans, or whether the British can achieve greater success than they did historically.

THE SIEGE

Given the relative strengths of the opposing armies and the nature of the British defences, a prolonged siege can have only one end. Even introducing a British relief force simply increases the problem of hiding men from the Allied guns, or alters it to one of a major evacuation in the presence of a numerically and logistically superior foe. However, a formal siege game – using rules such as Christopher Duffy's *Fire & Stone* – could be undertaken, with a British 'victory' dependent on how long they hold out, until either a relief force arrives, or the Allies are clearly ready to assault Yorktown. Extra 'time' can be bought by sorties and other ruses, but as the siege progresses, Cornwallis's men will become exhausted from having to maintain the defences, and their numbers will be reduced by disease and wounds. As a result, any activity they undertake will become less effective the longer the siege goes on; equally, the defences will deteriorate (from the actions of nature, as well as the enemy), leading to increased casualties from Allied artillery and providing a less daunting obstacle to any assault.

The game could be made less predictable by allowing Graves to capture or disperse the squadron carrying the French siege train, leaving the American guns to do all the work; or the Allies could be decimated by heat-stroke (to which the French were particularly susceptible) or disease, while constructing the siege works (some Americans believed Cornwallis had runaway slaves injected with small pox, then sent into the Allied camp).

A less formal alternative – requiring fewer figures and playing space – would be a game of the siege of Gloucester Point. Lacking the manpower and matériel to 'dig for victory', de Choisy planned a frontal assault only for the American militia to refuse to advance at the last minute. The irate de Choisy – who was very forthright in his opinions of Weedon – had to content himself with keeping the British penned inside their lines.

For those wanting conventional figure games, specific incidents from the siege, such as the cavalry battle at Gloucester Point, the feint attack on the Fusilier Redoubt, the night assaults on Redoubts No. 9 and No. 10, or Abercrombie's vain sortie could be recreated. Alternatively, some interesting 'what if' games could be based on a British decision to hold their outer line, rather than withdraw at once into Yorktown; a successful British attempt to evacuate to Gloucester and fight their way out past de Choisy; or an amphibious assault around either flank of the Allied force.

At a lower level, a role play game could be based on the experiences of the ordinary soldier (of either side) in the trenches during the siege. Some years ago, *Miniature Wargames* carried an article by Arthur Harman describing a game reproducing the personal experiences of an infantry unit at Waterloo, and this system could easily be adapted, using the memoirs of combatants. The 'unit' would be required to excavate (or repair) so much trench, and/or perform other tasks, while under fire; individuals might have specific tasks, such as 'shell spotting'.

FOOTNOTES

1 Four warships – HMS *Raisonable* (64), *Rainbow* (44), *Otter* (16), *Haarlem* (12), 16 transports, one galley, seven tenders; Royal Artillery (70 men, six 4-pdrs.), four Foot Guards' flank companies (390), 42nd Foot (500), light company 82nd Foot (50), Volunteers of Ireland (300), Prinz Karl Infantry Regiment (500).

2 Royal Artillery (20), all ten companies 80th Foot (730), Hessian Jaeger corps (125), Queen's Rangers (430), Loyal Americans (145), American Legion (35), guides/pioneers (65).

3 1st Light Battalion (477), 2nd Light Battalion (526), 43rd Foot (375), all ten companies 76th Foot (606), Erbprinz Infantry Regiment (502), Hessian artillery (34); in April, they were joined by five companies 17th Foot (274), 1st Anspach-Bayreuth Infantry Regiment (617), 2nd Anspach-Bayreuth Infantry Regiment (598).

4 Roughly equivalent to brigadier-generals in the British or American service, but mainly used as a pool of general officers available for special tasks, or the command of detached corps.

5 Contrary to popular myth, Continental infantry regiments were not filled with patriotic farmers and tradesmen with families; they were young (half were under 22 on enlistment), rootless, unskilled men, enlisting – often unwillingly – as paid substitutes, or to escape poverty and servitude. They were led by an officer corps from the upper strata of colonial society, who assumed command as naturally in war as they did in peace, and remained distant from their men as part of the disciplinary regime (though enlisted men were commissioned). Indeed, the Continentals hardly differed from the traditional stereotypes of the British regulars.

6 Coppering involved covering the hull of a ship below the waterline with strips of copper sheet to retard the encrusting of the hull by marine animals and plants which drastically reduced a ship's speed. As the design of French ships made them inherently faster than their British counterparts, Destouches' vessels must have been in a bad state.

7 On 9 May, the British post of Pensacola in West Florida had surrendered after a two-month siege to several thousand Spanish troops transported from Cuba by a Franco-Spanish fleet. Other matters, and the limited tactical importance of the post, seemed to prevent any appreciation that every unit of British troops in North America was in a similar position – too far from any other group for mutual support by land, surrounded by hostile countryside and a numerically superior foe, and totally reliant on local naval supremacy for food, military supplies, reinforcement and – most importantly – escape.

8 Although the absence of boats would prevent the French from taking possession of captured British ships, or abandoning their own if they sank, this did remove what was invariably an encumbrance on the deck of any fighting ship in action – as well as a major source of lethal flying splinters.

9 The Gatenois Regiment, formed from the junior half of the Royal Auvergne regiment some years earlier, was rewarded for its part in this action by being allowed to use their former title 'Auvergne sans tache' (without stain).

10 The Earl's absence – often commented on sarcastically by writers – may well have been genuine, as sickness had been rife in Cornwallis's army throughout the southern campaigns. Cornwallis himself had fallen ill with fever on at least two occasions, and the 42-year-old Earl, who had served continuously in the field since January 1780, also suffered from malaria.

11 As with so many famous images of this war, that of the British marching out of Yorktown with their band playing 'The World Turned Upside Down' is highly suspect. First, there was no 'band'; most, if not all, of the British and German regiments would have had a group of musicians (of distinctly variable quality and quantity). Second, each regimental band would have had a selection of favourite tunes, including regimental marches, and while there may have been some agreement to play the same tune, there was no official stipulation as to what should be played (except that it could not be a French or American tune, in retaliation for Lincoln's army at Charleston being forbidden to play a British one). Third, from Yorktown to the surrender field was over a mile (around 30 minutes' march), so a medley of tunes would most likely have been played. Fourth, observers recalled the playing as slow, mournful, even careless (some of the troops appeared drunk), but strangely there is no mention of such an appropriate tune; in fact, the only 'evidence' is a third-hand account published 40 years later, in a book of anecdotes. Finally, no such 'song' existed in 1781 (though there is an early 19th century nonsense song of that title); the phrase 'the world turned upside down' occurs in several songs of the period, but the melody associated with Yorktown traditionally accompanied another song, 'When the King enjoys his own again'. If some British musicians did play the tune, it was probably to suggest defiance and retribution – as any Americans present who recognised it may have guessed.

INDEX

(References to illustrations are shown in **bold**)